REVIVAL OR REJECTION!

Will we answer the call to take advantage of our times?

by

Rod Butterworth

Copyright © 2018 by Rod Butterworth

Please note the scriptures quoted are purposely given bold type as a personal preference from usual conventional standards.

Scriptures quotations are from the New King James Version Copyright © 1982 by Thomas Nelson, Inc., unless otherwise stated.

*TO MY WIFE LINDA,
OUR CHILDREN, GRANDCHILDREN,
AND THOSE WHO SEEK THE LORD
WITH ALL THEIR HEART*

"Revival in a nation like America must begin with God's professed believers. We must pray the prayer of repentance for the sins of our nation, and commit to radical witnessing with the love of God pouring forth from our hearts." RB

CONTENTS

1. IF MY PEOPLE
2. WHO ARE CALLED BY MY NAME
3. WILL HUMBLE THEMSELVES
4. AND PRAY
5. AND SEEK MY FACE
6. AND TURN FROM THEIR WICKED WAYS
7. THEN I WILL HEAR FROM HEAVEN
8. AND WILL FORGIVE THEIR SIN
9. AND HEAL THEIR LAND
10. BEING A PART OF GOD'S PLAN
11. BOUGHT TO SERVE
12. HIS LEADING NOT MINE
13. HIS POWER NOT MINE
14. HIS WORD WILL PREVAIL
15. THE POWER OF LIVING IN HIS LOVE
16. REVIVAL THROUGH RELATIONSHIP
17. EXTREME SACRIFICE?
18. WHAT WILL WE CHOOSE?

INTRODUCTION

It was 4.30 a.m. that the Holy Spirit woke me up on Thursday, April 6, 2017. More than once something like this has happened in my life when my spirit and mind were deeply stirred. I was tossing and turning on my bed with a powerful burden in my heart for the declining spiritual state of America.

In the pitch-black darkness of the bedroom I reached for the bedside table on which I had left a pad and pen for such occasions as this. I wanted to make sure I didn't forget this persistent inner voice coming to me through my spirit during this early morning hour. My hand touched a pair of reading glasses I had placed on the bedside table which made a little clatter. Next to me my wife stirred when she must have heard this. After trying to be more careful as I moved my hand around the smooth tabletop I still couldn't locate the pad and pen.

I laid back on my pillow for a moment thinking: I'll just wait a while because I'm surely not going to forget this dramatic inspirational awakening I was receiving from the Lord. But almost immediately I realized this was not going to work. My thoughts were aflame with the shocking words I was hearing in my mind: *"Revival or Rejection."* I got up, went across the hallway to my office, shut the door, and sat down in front of my laptop. I began typing. After writing this much, I stopped to kneel in front of my office sofa and began to seek the Lord in earnest prayer.

This is how the book you are now reading began. The day before my nighttime experience I heard a well-known conservative radio host say that if the time ever came when liberals outnumbered conservatives, America would be gone! I remember thinking as I heard this that another way to put it would be that if the unrighteous outnumbered the righteous in America, our future as Christians would very likely include severe persecution. Such a situation would surely take this country in the opposite direction from the intention of our godly nation's founders (those that were), and would be contrary to the very purpose for which America came into being—religious freedom based on biblical principles and the gospel of Jesus Christ. But then I remember the Bible accounts of minorities defeating majorities. The key is being on the right side! Yes, there is hope!

Revival or rejection! Was the Lord revealing to me His perspective on America as a nation, the nominal organized Church, the true body of Christ, or all three? Was there a need for America as a whole to regain any degree of spiritual righteousness which may have been lost? Obviously, yes. But how could such a dramatic change happen? Any Christian who knows the Bible well should be able to see that Satan, the enemy of God, has made huge inroads of ungodliness into our society—yes, that word *sin*. He has deceived millions and been able to successfully promote secular worldviews and practices that are anti-God and anti-Bible. Three of the most powerful anti-God influences promoted by Satan in America today include devaluing the sanctity of human life through abortion, humanistic evolutionary philosophy, and sexual immorality and perversions.

This book is a message for the Church—all who believe they have a living, saving relationship with God through faith in Jesus Christ. Our preachers, teachers and evangelists need to be aflame with powerful Holy-Spirit anointing of righteousness and uncompromising declaration of the Word of God. Such ministry should not only be within the Church, but through the bold witness of each one of us in the daily marketplace. Do Christians need to be full of the Spirit and holy zeal to be the powerful witnesses our Lord expects of His people similar to that of our brothers and sisters in the early Church? Absolutely! For the future of the body of Christ in America, I believe the Lord has shown me the days ahead will be either revival or rejection! People across America will likely be experiencing both at the same time! In this year of 2018 the political climate of America is changing dramatically since the installation of Donald Trump as president in 2017. These new circumstances reveal that a window of opportunity has opened up with the possibility of change for the better. Can America become great again as a godlier nation? Jonathan Cahn writes,

> "So in the present case the answer was not an election, a man, a party, or a political agenda. A political answer cannot solve a spiritual problem. But it can open a window through which that answer can come [revival]. On the other hand, a political turning without a corresponding spiritual turning will end up in failure or calamity [rejection]. As for the desire to make America great again, the only way America can be great again is for America to return to the God who made America great in the first place. The answer is repentance, return, and revival" (Jonathan Cahn. *The Paradigm*. Frontline, Charisma Media/Charisma House Book Group, Lake Mary, FL, 2017 221).

We have a great opportunity in these early days of the twenty-first century to see first-hand what God can do in answer to prayer. There are many great revival scriptures pastors and teachers have passionately preached and taught over the years, but one definitely stands out among others:

"If My people who are called by My name will humble themselves, and pray and seek My face, and turn from their wicked ways, then I will hear from heaven, and will forgive their sin and heal their land" (2 Chronicles 7:14).

CHAPTER 1

IF MY PEOPLE

When God refers to **"My people"** are you sure this includes you? You may be thinking: Why does this writer need to be so direct? I believe the Bible *is* very direct, and Jesus was certainly down-to-earth and specific when He taught there is only one way to heaven—through Him. Here is another straight-forward, powerful and eternal biblical truth: Only the forgiven and the forgiving will make it to heaven—those who can say with the Apostle John, that He has **"washed us from our sins in His own blood"** (Revelation 1:5). If there is someone you have not forgiven you will *not* be counted among those who **"shall be clothed in white raiment"** (Revelation 3:5 KJV), because these are exclusively only the ones who have overcome sin in their lives. In order to be *God's true people* we must forgive as we have been forgiven. It will be either personal revival or personal rejection.

When God says **"If"** there will be a minimum of two possible outcomes. A choice is implied. When we think back to the very beginning of humanity we know Adam and Eve were faced with a momentous choice. God allowed this test because He wanted all of us to reap the results of our own freewill choices. In His supernatural wisdom He created us with this awesome gift because He wanted a reciprocal relationship with the zenith of His creation—of course, us.

The independent choices God gives us the freedom to make will be either positive or negative, good or bad, and will lead us on a path to revival or rejection. The temptation Adam and Eve were confronted with and their response to it was infinitely crucial then, and has since affected all of humanity for time and eternity. God is loving and merciful, and deals with His creation through divine wisdom and justice. He does not want to treat us like helpless babies or puppets on a string, because that is not what we are expected to be in our relationship with Him.

The Bible is clear that He has given to us the responsibility to act upon His Word by using the wisdom and intelligence He makes available to us. He has created us in His image with gifts of creative genius and the choice to express that creativeness in various ways. It is always by *faith* that He expects us to interact with Him, and Scripture reveals that He has given all of us a sufficient measure of faith. Romans 12:3 confirms this when the Apostle Paul wrote, **"as God has dealt to each one a [the** KJV] **measure of faith.** However, as mentioned above, the "if" implies we can go in one of two directions—either according to His will, or by the will of our own choosing.

When He refers to us as **"My people"** it immediately tells us we are privileged to be in a unique and special relationship with Him. In other words, we are part of His spiritual family, the Church or body of Christ, where God the Father is the patriarch or head. But what kind of relationship? Although He may call us His people, the question arises as to whether we are in a close enough relationship with Him to be willing and obedient in carrying out His will. Are we really His faithful and obedient people or not? Do we respond with thanksgiving and praise for His loving care and provision we can all experience? Have we shown our love for Him by spending quality time with Him in prayer and meditation in the Word? Are our lives pleasing to Him in general—our thoughts, words and actions? Do we love the other members of His body as we should? Are we jealous for praise to be offered exclusively for the glory of God and the prosperity of His kingdom? Are we open and ready to share the Gospel with genuine intense love as we find opportunity? Do we have the same kind of compassion for the unsaved we see in the heart and ministry of Jesus as revealed through the gospel accounts? The Apostle Paul exhorts believers: **"Examine yourselves *as to* whether you are in the faith. Test yourselves. Do you not know yourselves, that Jesus Christ is in you?—unless indeed you are disqualified"** (2 Corinthians 13:5).

Putting it simply, we are either **"in the faith"** or we are **"disqualified."** We are either in revival mode or rejection mode. Professing Christians are deceived if they think they can stand on the fence of neutrality. Attempting to be neutral would be equal to not being **"in the faith."** Also, claiming to be in a supposed neutral state of spiritual limbo would obviously not bode well for one's future. With God it is all or nothing as far as the condition and state of our personal relationship with Him is concerned. We are either totally on His side or we are deceiving ourselves. Jesus said, **"He who is not with Me is against Me"** (Matthew 12:30).

The word **"disqualified"** (Greek, *adokimos*) signifies not standing the test, rejected (W. E. Vine, *An Expository Dictionary* 1966 p. 173). The same word is translated *reprobate mind* in the King James Version (Romans 1:28). The charge to **"Examine yourselves"** implies the possibility that persons who think they are **"in the faith"** may be shocked to find out they are not. What does it mean to be *in the faith*? It means experiencing a living, active, intimately personal, obedient, consistent saving faith relationship with the Lord throughout the days of our lives.

The phrase **"If My people"** reminds us that we do not belong to ourselves. No, the Bible tells us we have been bought with a price, and we are not our own. Have we followed the example of Jesus by surrendering our will obediently to God as Jesus did in the Garden of Gethsemane when He said, **"Nevertheless, not as I will, but as You** *will"* (Matthew 26:39). If we think we can pray for revival but have not totally surrendered our wills to Him, our prayers will not be answered. However, our possession by God and our submission to Him is not a negative thing—but will be to our eternal benefit, because the way through which we become His possession is by a voluntary choice on our part.

To illustrate: Probably many of us would think that to be born into a financially wealthy family with all our material needs met would conjure up a rather pleasant scenario. But in such a situation it should cause us to have a sense of responsibility to be good representatives of the family, and keep the family name honored, respected and appreciated. How much more, then, should not those of us born into the family of God— by our own choice in believing (through the gift of grace and faith)—be conscious of the need to actively promote the name and heritage of this spiritual family? Are we really committed to being active loyal members of the family of God or not?

Because of my deep concern for our nation I feel the need for honest evaluation of the spiritual condition of the family of God, the Church, in America today. How many believe themselves to be included among the **"My people"** of our main text? How many of us who claim to be Christians have a real personal continual daily relationship with Him? What a shock it would be if we came to the realization that God may be rejecting us. The people of Israel in Old Testament times had confidence they were God's people when they served Him with sincerity of heart. But there were times in their history when they did not have a genuine relationship with Him.

Having a genuine relationship with Him means we are experiencing real-time daily fellowship and interaction with Him. An example from Ezekiel 33:31 tells of a time when the people of Jerusalem were not taking Ezekiel's ministry seriously. It reads:

"So they come to you as people do, they sit before you *as* My people, and they hear your words, but they do not do them; for with their mouth they show much love, *but* their hearts pursue their *own* gain."

Could there be church congregations in America whose visible expressions of church involvement are similar to the situation in Ezekiel's day? Could there be churches existing today that are rejected by God and don't know it? Sadly, absolutely! Jeremiah the prophet also painfully describes the sad condition of those in His day who saw themselves as God's chosen people. Terrible times had visited Israel. Jerusalem had been literally destroyed and the people had been taken captive or scattered by the Babylonian invaders. He writes:

"The joy of our heart has ceased; Our dance has turned into mourning. The crown has fallen *from* our head. Woe to us, for we have sinned! Because of this our heart is faint; Because of these *things* our eyes grow dim; Because of Mount Zion which is desolate, with foxes walking about on it. Turn us back to You, O Lord, and we will be restored; Renew our days as of old, unless You have utterly rejected us, *and* are very angry with us!" (Lamentations 5:15-18; 21-22).

The first thing Jeremiah mentions is the lack of joy among the people of God. Any celebrations they used to relish and enjoy have long ceased. When souls are saved today with genuine repentance it is certainly a cause for great rejoicing, but so many American churches (not all, thank God) have not seen such things happen for years. New converts are rare. Most additions to the number of people attending congregations are by birth or change of address. Therefore, the lack of real spiritual joy and effective ministry in churches today must be an indication of something extremely important missing. It would surely point to evidence of an unhealthy relationship with God, resulting in a lack of spiritual vitality. Jesus said, **"These things I have spoken to you, that My joy may remain in you, and *that* your joy may be full"** (John 15:11). Are we living this by experience?

Jeremiah writes that the heart of the people **"is faint."** Many of our churches in America have become progressively weak or faint, especially over the last sixty years. Even though some denominations can point to new church buildings and a measure of growth, Christian influence in our culture has diminished as evidenced by the corollary evil of ungodliness we see prevalent and growing in our culture today.

As an immigrant from England to this country over fifty years ago, I have sadly watched a decline take place in the political, economic, social, religious and biblical spiritual values upon which America was founded. For example: Has the Church as a whole actively voiced their resistance to the horrendous God-denying ugly sins of abortion and sexual perversions? There are so-named and self-professed Christians who not only give their support to these evils, but even volitionally and gladly allow such influences to infiltrate their churches—even to the extent of ordaining known sexually immoral persons to the ministry. And we wonder why the impact of today's churches in American culture is as weak as it is! A spiritual erosion has taken place. There are **"foxes walking about"** on the crumbling walls and remains of previously strong spiritual defenses. There are those who claim to be servants of the Lord, but who need to be exposed for what they really are, and should be called to account for what they are doing that is contrary to biblical truth. Surely we should be confessing along with Jeremiah: **"Woe to us, for we have sinned!"**

Jeremiah knows the answer to the problems plaguing the people of God. He writes: **"Turn us back to You, O Lord, and we will be restored."** The way to recovery is by a restoration of the relationship between God and His people. If we, in America, are honest enough to confess our lack of intimate relationship with God and cry out to Him in sincerity for restoration, He will hear and answer such a prayer.

Jeremiah also prayed, **"Renew our days as of old."** Along this line we can think of the dedication of those first disciples of Jesus who **"turned the world upside down"** (Acts 17:6). Even though this was stated by those who were very much in opposition, the truth remains that the disciples' witness of the Gospel was powerfully affecting their culture, as it should. Let's face it, we have had it too easy in America. The Church has gone to sleep in many ways and has not been the light and salt of influence it is called to be for the Lord. If this condition continues to prevail without change there will be much difficulty and challenge in the days ahead. There could even be rejection! Yes, Jeremiah wrote of the possibility of God's people being rejected with these words:

"Renew our days as of old, unless You have utterly rejected us, *and* are very angry with us!" (Lamentations 5:21,22).

Some may be thinking: Surely God would not reject His Church today. God is a God of love, and He knows all about our weaknesses and will overlook the mistakes we are making. After all, we all fail in various ways. Yet, Jeremiah does raise the possibility of rejection as a real act of God's judgment. Some might say that things are different today because we are under grace and not under law (beware of unscriptural *antinomian hyper grace* as taught by some today). So we need to turn to Jesus for a moment and learn from Him about His relationship with the Church. This is what He said about two of the first century churches concerning their spiritual condition:

"Remember therefore from where you have fallen; repent and do the first works, or else I will come to you quickly and remove your lampstand from its place—unless you repent" (Revelation 2:5).

The phrase **"remove your lampstand from its place"** is a serious warning indeed. Revelation 1:20 tells us that **"the seven lampstands which you saw are the seven churches."** So what does Jesus mean when He says He will remove their lampstand from its place? It can only mean that His relationship with the church at Ephesus would be severed—they would be rejected. Donald Stamps writes:

> "Christ will remove any congregation or church from its place and destiny in God's kingdom if it has lost its true passion and purpose for God and does not repent and renew its love for and obedience to the Lord Jesus Christ" (Donald C. Stamps. Life Publishers International: Springfield, MO. MEV note 2;5. 2015 1914).

What was the root of this church's problem? Jesus said, **"Nevertheless I have this against you, that you have left you first love. Remember therefore from where you have fallen; repent and do the first works"** (Revelation 2:4,5). They failed in the one thing that was most important to the Lord, they didn't love Him passionately, and therefore could not be considered *His people* in the proper sense. They had forgotten to obey the greatest and most important commandment which says: **"The first of all the commandments is: Hear, O Israel, the Lord our God, the Lord is one. And you shall love the Lord your God with all your heart, with all your soul, with all your mind, and with all your strength"** (Mark 12:29,30).

The reason we exist and the reason God created the entire cosmos, is because above everything else He desires a one-on-one personal relationship with each of us. We are not *His people* just because we attend a church service in a church building somewhere. Neither are we *His people* if we merely engage in good works, pay tithes to support the Church, and have even labored for **"My name's sake and have not become weary"** (Revelation 2:3). No, we can only be *His people* in the fullest sense if we are in a continual personal love relationship with Him. Consider the words of Jesus to the church at Laodicea:

"I know your works, that you are neither cold nor hot. I could wish you were cold or hot. So then, because you are lukewarm, and neither cold nor hot, I will vomit you out of My mouth" (Revelation 3:15,16).

Is this really Jesus speaking? Is it possible that He could say something so seemingly harsh and judgmental? Absolutely! But actually, Jesus was speaking with love in His heart for the Laodiceans because correction was needed for their own good. It is time we, the Church, get serious about the wonderful grace God has bestowed upon us, and seek His wisdom with reverential fear in order to be the people He has called us to be as His servants. Proverbs 9:10 says,

"The fear of the Lord is the beginning of wisdom,

and the knowledge of the Holy One is understanding."

The challenge remains for all of us who claim a relationship with the Lord to examine ourselves and discover whether or not we are really *His people*. I believe God could supernaturally influence us if He chose to do so in order to bend and shape us to perform His will. But instead He chooses to wait for us to willingly follow His way rather than our own. A man came to visit our museum who claimed to be an agnostic—one who thinks there may be a God who created but who now has nothing to do with His creation personally. Imagine how such thinking must be grieving to God when the evidence for His existence and care of this planet is evident everywhere.

However, as true Christians born from above by His Spirit we have already experienced His love and grace, and we should be very attentive to any words of direction or commands He makes known to us. This is what true family members are supposed to do. We are to show special respect and honor to the One who has received us into fellowship with Himself. In other words, God has the perfect right to give us promises based on conditions that He sets. If we fulfill the condition or conditions, we can always expect God to do His part. So the phrase **"If My people"** speaks of a condition for us to implement with the knowledge of a promise to follow. The question is, are we of the right mind and heart to actively enter into this opportunity to see the Lord do wonders in answer to our obedience? Is the spiritual future of America worth it?

In the next chapter we will see what it means to be identified with the name of God.

CHAPTER 2

WHO ARE CALLED BY MY NAME

Names are important. Most of us would not think of changing our family name and its connection with our ancestors. One of my daughters thought it would be interesting to have a DNA ancestry test to find out more about her family biological history, and has persuaded me to do the same. This can certainly be interesting, but the biblical truth is that all humans are related. The Bible account of the Flood in Noah's day about 4,500 years ago reminds us we are all descended from Noah, his three sons and their wives.

By going back to the beginning we discover that in a unique sense we are all related to our Creator God himself, because we would not be here if He had not imparted His breath of life into Adam's newly created body. We are a worldwide family! There is only one race—the human race. We have all received the same breath of physical life that began with Adam. Genesis 2:7 reads: **"And the Lord God formed man *of* the dust of the ground, and breathed into his nostrils the breath of life; and man became a living being [soul KJV]."**

Since God created us we cannot get away from the fact that He is our history and the reason we exist. But the question arises: Have we identified ourselves personally with Him, by coming into a relationship with Him and His name through the means He has provided through faith in Jesus Christ, and His sacrifice on the cross? Would people in our circle of acquaintances know by their contact with us that we are identified with the name of Jesus Christ? Have we of our own choosing willingly aligned ourselves personally with the God who created us, and have we recognized our responsibility to come to Him and be united with Him through faith? Do we identify ourselves, our unique individuality and our persona as being under that name—the name of God the Father, Jesus the Son, and the Holy Spirit?

In general, professed Christians would answer these questions affirmatively. There is no privilege more sublime than being identified with the name of God. We should be jealous for the respect and honor that should always be given to our Lord's name, and should be bold enough to speak up for it when the occasion demands it. For example, if someone in our presence takes the name of the Lord in vain accompanied with cursing, we should be bold enough to lovingly suggest that such is not appropriate.

Jesus instructed us to pray with the words, **"Our Father in heaven, hallowed be Your name"** (Matthew 6:9). The word **"hallowed"** is from the Greek root *hagios* which means: made holy or sacred; to venerate; and to give the greatest respect and honor. Christians have been given the awesome privilege and right to call on the name of the Lord when coming to Him with their prayers and petitions. Jesus said: **"And whatever you ask in My name, that I will do, that the Father may be glorified in the Son. If you ask anything in My name, I will do *it*"** (John 14:13,14).

If we are truly among those who are **"called by My name"** we should have a deep passionate desire to faithfully lift up that name through our personal witness. We should literally be willing to lay down our lives in service for the honor of representing that name, and I'm sure my discerning readers do not think such could never happen in America. According to news reports there are millions of believers currently (2018) being martyred for their Christian faith. It is open season on persecuting Christians in many places around the world, and we should be willing to accept God's plan for each of us individually should persecution come our way. With such a commitment we will fulfill His calling upon our lives and the crucial part each of us should play in seeking God diligently for a spiritual awakening in our land.

As representatives of God with the privilege and authority in using His name, we should be doing everything possible under His leading to be faithful and persistent in our prayers for revival and restoration of righteousness in America. Our attitude should be that we dare not cease praying as we expect the Holy Spirit to do His work among precious souls by bringing them into the kingdom of God. God has done it in the past, and we know He can do it again. The Apostle Paul actually wrote the words, **"Pray without ceasing"** (1 Thessalonians 5:17), which seems to be impractical at first reading. But I believe he meant that we should be ready for our lips to utter prayer at any time, and this should be a lifelong commitment.

Genesis 3: 20 reads: **"And Adam called his wife's name Eve, because she was the mother of all living."** After God had created Eve out of Adam's side and brought her to him, we read that Adam said, **"This is now bone of my bones and flesh of my flesh; She shall be called Woman** (Hebrew, *Ishshah*), **because she was taken out of Man** (Hebrew, *Ish*). So we can see from the beginning of creation that both God and Adam recognized as important the identification of individual names.

I believe it to be true that Christians often forget during the hours of each day that God wants to interact individually with them. After all, by comparison the Bible tells us God even **"counts the number of the stars; He calls them all by name"** (Psalm 147:4). Stars are made up of chemical gasses and matter with no life in them. If

God gives individual names to the billions of stars in the galaxies of the heavens, He surely knows the name of everyone who has ever lived on this planet. Apparently God respects the names given to people on earth until the time comes when victorious overcoming believers will receive a new name in heaven (Revelation 2:17).

Genesis 12:2 records God's promise to Abraham: **I will make you a great nation; I will bless you and make your name great; and you shall be a blessing. I will bless those who bless you, and I will curse him who curses you; and in you all the families of the earth shall be blessed."** Abraham received this great promise from God who told him his name would be made great. We might be tempted to think Abraham was special and therefore we cannot expect God to pay that kind of attention to us as individual Christians today.

Abraham was indeed special, but so is everyone special and unique in the eyes of God. The Apostle Peter said, **"Of a truth I perceive that God is no respecter of persons. But in every nation he that feareth him, and worketh righteousness, is accepted with him"** (KJV Acts 10:34,35). Jesus said, **"Look at the birds of the air, for they neither sow nor reap nor gather into barns; yet your heavenly Father feeds them. Are you not of more value than they?** (Matthew 6:26). And, **"But the very hairs of your head are all numbered"** (Matthew 10:30).

Therefore, with these truths in mind we should be awestruck with the realization of a very real and personal link between each of us as individuals and our wonderful Lord, the Creator of the universe. He knows our names, and gives us the privilege of knowing Him by His name. He is especially interested in our welfare as members of His inner circle of believers. Psalm 91 is well known to most Christians, and gives us some exciting promises related to our intimate relationship with Him. Referring to the believer it reads:

"Because he has set his love upon Me, therefore I will deliver him; I will set him on high, because he has known My name. He shall call upon Me, and I will answer him; I *will* be with him in trouble; I will deliver him and honor him. With long life I will satisfy him, and show him My salvation" (Psalm 91:14-16).

Deliverance from unrighteousness and sinful lifestyles is desperately needed in America—and not just among unbelievers! We are in serious trouble and have seen the pendulum of influence swinging more and more to the liberal ungodly side. But the verse quoted above has the answer, that is, if we the people of His name will actively do what He tells us to do. The first challenge is this: Have we really set our love upon Him? How do we go about doing this?

First, if you really love someone you will want to spend time with that one. Are we representing the name of our God well if our interest is mainly in materialistic things and enjoyment in secular entertainment, with little time spent in private communion with Him? So how do we begin? Prayer! What an inexpressible privilege it is that we are invited to have personal contact with the One who created us. But are we doing it—daily? The promise in the scripture above includes the blessing of experiencing deliverance in any areas of our lives where such is needed. This will set us free and enable us to have a powerful testimony and witness to others.

Second, the clause **"I will set him on high"** tells believers God will provide special supernatural protection. Matthew Henry writes: "That he will exalt and dignify them: *I will set him on high*, out of the reach of trouble, above the stormy region, on a rock *above the* *waves*" (*The Matthew Henry Commentary.* Zondervan Publishing House, Grand Rapids. 1978 678).

But what about America? Has our nation been set on high above trouble, violence, and degeneration? We know the sad and obvious answer only too well. America is in dire need of a spiritual awakening, for it is at the level of individual hearts where change for the better must begin. Many prominent Christians are saying the same thing. Billy Graham's son Franklin has stated that the only hope for America is prayer.

Satan has been very active and clever in causing outright unbelief in God, the Bible, and all things related to righteousness—especially since the early 1960s. So what is the answer? Where do we go from here? We must put active faith with appropriate action in the promise contained in Psalm 91:5:

"He shall call upon Me, and I will answer him; I *will be* with him in trouble; I will deliver him and honor him."

We have to do the calling. If we call upon Him the promise confirms He will answer us, be with us, deliver us and honor us. Since we are called by His name (as Christians) we must take advantage of our relationship with Him and put into practice the means He has provided for us to implement. Even when we are in trouble, as America is now, He has promised to be with us if we will faithfully trust Him to remedy the situation.

The only way to see America changing with improvement toward a godlier nation is for us, God's people, to seek His face in earnest. The future of America rests on the outcome of the choice indicated by the word **"If."** Conditions will either turn one way or the other. God is always willing to do His part if we are willing to do ours. If things became so evil that Christians everywhere in America were being put into prison for their faith, would there be enough evidence about your life and mine to qualify for such persecution? We should all examine our spiritual state to see if we are really a true representative of *that name*. Next, we will discover whether we are humble enough to admit our need.

CHAPTER 3

WILL HUMBLE THEMSELVES

We have all been guilty of the wrong kind of pride at various times in our lives. There is something embedded in our inner being—we could name it as our inherited sinful nature—that never wants to admit being wrong. Even when we know deep down we are wrong it is still extremely difficult to admit it. For example: Having been involved in the biblical creation ministry for many years, I sympathize with many who have been taught Darwinian evolution as a fact, and therefore would naturally be resistant and dismayed to think it possible they had been taught falsehoods. Most would just not want to believe it, and would continue to trust in what they had been taught.

It is not easy to change direction from the history of our upbringing and education. After all, those who have been our teachers during our developing years were supposed to be proficient in what they were teaching. But have those who wore the teacher's mantle (especially in secular education) really examined the foundation of what they have taught to see if it has validity? So when it comes to evaluating the cultural environment of America and the way it has molded and shaped our values, how do we know what the answers are to counteract the degeneration of our society?

Unfortunately, some would not even see the need to reset any supposed degeneration of society, especially with any involvement from religion. With pride in the ability to fix things without God they would cite things like better education and politics as solutions—in spite of the dismal failure in these areas. However, the Scripture we are considering in these chapters tells us where to begin, and this chapter reminds us of the need to humble ourselves before God and seek Him in earnest.

As mentioned above, pride can be a serious problem for all of us. Here are some of God's thoughts on pride:

Pride *goes* before destruction, and a haughty spirit before a fall (Proverbs 16:18).

When pride comes, then comes shame; but with the humble *is* wisdom (Proverbs 11:2).

By pride comes nothing but strife, but with the well-advised *is* wisdom (Proverbs 13:10).

A man's pride will bring him low, but the humble in spirit will retain honor (Proverbs 29:23).

The pride of your heart has deceived you, *You* who dwell in the clefts of the rock, Whose habitation is high; *You* who say in your heart, 'Who will bring me down to the ground?' (Obadiah 1:3).

For all that *is* in the world—the lust of the flesh, the lust of the eyes, and the pride of life—is not of the Father but is of the world (1 John 2:16).

I am my own worst enemy, is a thought most of us would have to admit contains a lot of truth. How many times has personal pride risen up in our emotions and led us into less than pleasant scenarios? One of the big culprits can be education—even though it is a blessing and a privilege to have had the opportunity to learn what is necessary for life and work, it can also be a deceptive source of unprofitable self-deception. Having myself been through more college and university education over the years than the average person, I know by personal experience how easy it is to fall into the trap of thinking more highly of oneself than one should.

When someone says something such as: You are so knowledgeable about this subject, and I admire your ability to talk about it; the emotional feeling of pride can very easily rise from within. We can quickly elevate ourselves in our own minds above what we actually are in reality. This cannot please God. It can certainly have the opposite effect of keeping our thinking balanced with a measure of humility.

Another problem that is related to the differences between the sexes, is the perception on one hand of the manliness of men, which does not seem to fit at first glance with the attitude of humility. The image of the macho man portrays someone who is independently in control of himself, perhaps others, and his relationship with them. On the other hand, a woman who may be told: I think you are very beautiful. You must have great discipline to keep yourself in such good shape; may find pride in her outward appearance a real hindrance to keeping the humble spirit.

So all of us face the challenge to live with a humble heart in our attitude and interaction with others. But if we would meditate more often on the greatness of God and His incomprehensible omnipotence (all power) and omniscience (all knowledge) compared to our own individual lives, I believe it would help us to see ourselves with more realistic eyes. To have reverential fear of the Lord and a prideful spirit do not mix. Hezekiah is an example from the Old Testament of a king (what a temptation to pride this would be just in itself to be a king) who found himself in an extremely dangerous life and death situation. He prayed, and God gave him and the people of Jerusalem a great victory against their enemies. But later, Hezekiah allowed pride to creep in. However, after some time he once again realized his mistake and knew what he needed to do. We read:

> **Then Hezekiah humbled himself for the pride of his heart, he and the inhabitants of Jerusalem, so that the wrath of the LORD did not come upon them in the days of Hezekiah** (2 Chronicles 32:26).

Note the phrase **"wrath of the LORD."** This verse is very appropriate for the subject we are considering. Because of Hezekiah's decision to humble himself the **"wrath of the LORD"** was averted. Could it be that America might be in danger of experiencing God's wrath and anger because of our ungodly society? Is it possible that the Lord is angry with America in general? I say, in general, because I believe there are many righteous godly people living in this country. But when we are honest with the spiritual state of America we should have much cause for alarm and concern. In my book *Found Wanting: America Needs Revival Now!* I wrote:

> America has never been in more danger than it is today in the teen years of this twenty-first century. It is as though this nation is standing on the edge of a dangerous precipice, where one more step would plunge it downward to certain destruction. Why does America find itself in such an alarming predicament? What has led up to America now standing on this precarious ledge of potential disaster when this nation has obviously been so greatly blessed in the past?
>
> A Christian might cry out in agonizing realization: Why have things changed so much for the worse? Why does there seem to be no stopping of political, economic, spiritual and moral decline of our nation?
>
> There are certainly many sensible and logical answers to these questions, but I believe the

bottom line has to do with our nation's relationship with God. Such was the problem in the days of Daniel when God declared to the ungodly king that he was **"weighed in the balances, and found wanting"** (Daniel 5:27). So where does America stand today in the eyes of God? (Rod Butterworth. *Found Wanting: America Needs Revival Now!* 2016 1).

How did Hezekiah deal with the crisis he faced? He **"humbled himself for the pride of his heart"** and prayed. This is what our main theme verse from second Chronicles would tell us should be our response to the spiritual needs of America. If the spiritual condition of a nation is as it should be, things can begin to move in the right direction to correct the problems that afflict our society. Yes, the prayers offered in humility will have tremendous life-changing effect. But humility is so often that elusive quality which seems to dissipate as soon as we think about it. Let's look at the One who demonstrated true humility as recorded in Scripture.

"Let this mind be in you which was also in Christ Jesus, who, being in the form of God, did not consider it robbery to be equal with God, but made Himself of no reputation, taking the form of a bondservant, *and* **coming in the likeness of men. And being found in appearance as a man, He humbled Himself and became obedient to** *the point of* **death, even the death of the cross.**

Therefore God also has highly exalted Him and given Him the name which is above every name, that at the name of Jesus every knee should bow, of those in heaven, and of those on earth, and of those under the earth, and *that* **every tongue should confess that Jesus Christ** *is* **Lord, to the glory of God the Father"** (Philippians 2:5-11).

"Therefore whoever humbles himself as this little child is the greatest in the kingdom of heaven" (Matthew 18:4).

Jesus, is the perfect example of humility in wonderful balance with who He was as the divine Son of God. What unbelievable grace it took for Jesus to be willing to identify Himself with sinful mankind. If we could imagine ourselves in a similar position of spiritual royalty and power as Jesus, would we have been willing to do as He did? We know why He did it. Putting the most profound act of the universe in simple explanatory terms, He loves us and wants to provide salvation for us so we can spend eternity with Him in glorious fellowship. He tells us we should take notice of a child's humble innocence to understand what He is looking for in us as His people. Jesus gives us an illustration by example of the difference between the prideful spirit and the humble spirit. We read:

"Two men went up to the temple to pray, one a Pharisee and the other a tax collector. The Pharisee stood and prayed thus with himself, 'God, I thank You that I am not like other men—extortioners, unjust, adulterers, or even as this tax collector. I fast twice a week; I give tithes of all I possess.'

And the tax collector, standing afar off, would not so much as raise *his* eyes to heaven, but beat his breast, saying 'God, be merciful to me a sinner!' I tell you, this man went down to his house justified *rather* than the other; for everyone who exalts himself will be humbled, and he who humbles himself will be exalted" (Luke 18:10-14).

Pride can be extremely deceptive. The Pharisee compared himself with others, and by doing so believed he was more pleasing to God. American Christians can easily fall into the same trap. We may think we are pleasing God like the Pharisee because we attend church and give one-tenth of our income to the ministry. We tend to pay attention to the outward tangible things when God is far more interested in the inner spiritual condition of the heart. Jesus spoke of His contemporaries with these words from Isaiah: **"These people draw near to Me with their mouth, and honor Me with their lips, but their heart is far from Me"** (Matthew 15:8). And Proverbs 4:23 advises: **"Keep your heart with all diligence, for out of it *spring* the issues of life."** And again in Proverbs 22:4: **"By humility and the fear of the Lord *are* riches and honor and life."**

True humility will get God's attention. We must learn to pray this dangerous prayer: Lord, show me myself as You see me. Yes, we may be shocked when He does, but this might be the starting point for many of us to begin positioning ourselves before God with the right attitude. The Apostle Peter wrote:

"Therefore humble yourselves under the mighty hand of God, that He may exalt you in due time" (1 Peter 5:6).

Notice that we are to **"humble ourselves."** This is something we are responsible for individually. I don't think we would enjoy the experience of God humbling us, although He may even do this in His love for us by chastising us at times when we need it (See Hebrews 12:5-9). Along this line I sometimes pray: Lord, please tread on my toes when necessary. We need to be totally honest with ourselves and open to the Lord's correction. This will inevitably involve change in our daily lives and interaction with others. The Apostle John recorded an amazing example of an act of humility by Jesus:

Jesus, knowing that the Father had given all things into His hands, and that He had come from

God and was going to God, rose from supper and laid aside His garments, took a towel and girded Himself. After that, He poured water into a basin and began to wash the disciples' feet, and to wipe *them* with the towel with which He was girded. Then He came to Simon Peter. And *Peter* said to Him, "Lord, are You washing my feet?"

Jesus answered and said to him, "What I am doing you do not understand now, but you will know after this."

Peter said to Him, "You shall never wash my feet!"

Jesus answered him, "If I do not wash you, you have no part with Me."

Simon Peter said to Him, "Lord, not my feet only, but also *my* hands and *my* head!"

Jesus said to him, "He who is bathed needs only to wash *his* feet, but is completely clean; and you are clean, but not all of you." For He knew who would betray Him; therefore He said, "You are not all clean."

So when He had washed their feet, taken His garments, and sat down again, He said to them, "Do you know what I have done to you? You call Me Teacher and Lord, and you say well, for *so* I am. If I then, *your* Lord and Teacher, have washed your feet, you also ought to wash one another's feet. For I have given you an example, that you should do as I have done to you. Most assuredly, I say to you, a servant is not greater than his master; nor is he who is sent greater than he who sent him. If you know these things, blessed are you if you do them" (John 13:3-17).

How would you feel if Jesus appeared to you and began to wash your feet? Would you react like Peter and say: This is not right? Yet Jesus did this wonderful act of humility to teach us by example. But in order for such acts of humility to be genuine they must spring from a heart of love. Jesus demonstrated true transparent love for the disciples in this very powerful way. Yes, humility is a big deal. If we don't have humility we will not be ready to engage in the all-important next step—prayer.

CHAPTER 4

AND PRAY

Do you pray? Is prayer an important part of your life? Would the actual time you give to prayer reveal something about how important it is to you? Are your prayer times exciting and awesome to you as you realize you are actually communicating personally with your Creator? The Bible tells us God will always hear and answer the sincere prayer of faith. We should surely consider it absolutely incredible and amazing that believing prayer can bring actual change not only to our own lives but also to the lives of others. The prayers of God's people can even change the course of nations.

But do most Christians really pray? There will be no revival without consistent, earnest, passionate prayer by true followers of Christ. Here's a fact based on biblical principles: America will not experience a spiritual awakening to any degree until millions of individual Christians become personally revived and learn to pray effectively. And if we don't pray we will likely experience some form of rejection!

Past revivals indicate it is generally *individual* revival being experienced first that leads to spiritual moves of God to produce community, city-wide, and possibly national revival. Do we really desire to see America's population more godly with worldviews based on biblical values and principles of righteousness? If we do we *must* pray. This is the divine order and biblical principle of God's directive to His people for spiritual renewal. But what kind of prayer? And how should we pray? Does the Bible give any instructions for praying effectively?

The practice of consistent prayer is one of the greatest privileges we have as Christians. If we do not avail ourselves of this awesome privilege we will lose many opportunities to see God at work through the answers to our prayers. But how much time does the average Christian spend in prayer? Andrew Murray, who wrote many devotional books to challenge and encourage believers to a deeper walk with God, wrote:

> "What use do we make of this heavenly privilege? How many there are who take only five minutes for prayer! They say that they have not time and that the heart desire for prayer is lacking; they do not *know how* to spend half an hour with God! It is not that they absolutely do not pray; they pray every day—but they have no joy in prayer, as a token of communion with God which shows that God is everything to them.
>
> If a friend comes to visit them, they have time, they *make time,* even at the cost of sacrifice, for the sake of enjoying converse with him. Yes, they have time for everything that really interests them, but not time to practice fellowship with God and delight themselves in Him! They find time for a creature who can be of service to them; but day after day, month after month passes, and there is no time to spend *one hour* with God" (Andrew Murray. *The Prayer Life.* Moody Press, Chicago. 1982 16).

In the Book of Genesis chapter three we learn that in the particular form He chose to reveal Himself, God spent time in personal relationship and communion with Adam and Eve every day. I'm sure Adam and Eve looked forward to this special time with great anticipation, and found these encounters with God extremely enjoyable—surely an understatement. Realizing *God's desire for fellowship with us* as revealed from those early days in the Garden of Eden, how do *our desires for fellowship with Him* compare today?

I sense more self-examination would seem necessary for most of us including myself on this matter. Do we look forward with great anticipation to our time spent with God each day? Do we have a great desire for these secret prayer trysts? Do we feel the excitement rise up in our hearts when we know we are about to begin our time alone with Him? Are we really willing to set aside enough time to have a meaningful personal relationship with the Lord? Do we sense a loss if we go through a day without that quiet time in His presence?

As seen from our vantage point on earth, time is passing as the sun moves across the sky. The seconds continue their relentless ticking from the moment we are born. No one has more time allotted than anyone else. But what can we do if our current schedules are making it very difficult to plan a reasonable time of private prayer? We may say our lives are just too busy and we don't know how we could change our daily activities. However, the Bible has something to say about the difficulties of managing our time:

And He said to them, "Come aside by yourselves to a deserted place and rest a while." For there were many coming and going, and they did not even have time to eat (Mark 6:31).

Jesus and His disciples were so overwhelmed with active ministry they didn't even have time to eat! So what was the solution to this seemingly out-of-control situation? It was simple! Drop what they were doing and purposely plan an actual physical escape from the busyness of their ministry. The lesson for us today is that we may at times have to make what some may see as unpopular inconvenient and drastic decisions. We *will* do this to give ourselves space for what is really important to us. Not only important, but vital when it comes to the crucial matter and necessity of personal private prayer!

At this time in our history America is in desperate need of faithful intercessors. Immorality, sacrilege, blasphemy, and evil in many forms have gained deceptive inroads into the hearts and lives of so many. Whatever the particular religious beliefs of America's founding fathers were, they would surely be shocked beyond belief to learn of the downward spiral that has already plunged areas of our culture into depths of depravity. Even if we have good Christian political leaders we should not expect them to be the ones to bring about a spiritual renewal.

The *only hope* for America to regain the favor of God is by the convicting power of the Holy Spirit to change the hearts of our people one by one. Such a revival, as has happened in the past, would greatly help to reestablish this nation on biblical principles and turn the tide of our culture from ungodliness toward righteousness. This is urgently needed in order to counteract the spiritual decline we have observed over the last 60 years. When we see the hearts of men and women in our culture continually drawn toward evil and ungodly lifestyles, the only hope for change is the spiritual renewal of our population one person at a time.

As mentioned above, we certainly cannot look to godly political leaders, if we should have them, to bring about such beneficial cultural change. Passing righteous laws based on biblical principles is a good thing, but not the complete answer. The real solution for renewal always starts with decisive action by God's dedicated people who are true believers. While the world uses their time to engage in secular pursuits without a thought of God, we, as God's people, should be weeping at the altars of individual and corporate prayer times for mercy and the salvation of these precious souls. Yes, it is the action of persistent passionate prayer that is needed, and concerned Christians must find time to pray daily. The Apostle Paul wrote:

"See then that you walk circumspectly [carefully], not as fools but as wise, redeeming the time, because the days are evil (Ephesians 5:15,16).

"Walk in wisdom toward those *who are* outside, redeeming the time" (Colossians 4:5).

The phrase **"redeeming the time"** means *making the most of,* or, *taking full advantage of time.* Yet, as we all know, it is so easy to let the seconds, minutes, and hours slip by as we live through each day. Distractions, distractions, distractions! King Solomon wrote this poetic passage about the use of time:

"To every *thing there is* a season, and a time to every purpose under the heaven: A time to be born, and a time to die; a time to plant, and a time to pluck up *that which* is planted; A time to kill, and a time to heal; a time to break down, and a time to build up; A time to weep, and a time to laugh; a time to mourn, and a time to dance; A time to cast away stones, and a time to gather stones together; a time to embrace, and a time to refrain from embracing; A time to get, and a time to lose; a time to keep, and a time to cast away; A time to rend, and a time to sew; a time to keep silence, and a time to speak; A time to love, and a time to hate; a time of war, and a time of peace" (Ecclesiastes 3:1-8 KJV).

Imagine if Jesus were to actually physically appear to us how we would explain our lack of prayer? Yes, such a thought suddenly elevates the matter of prayer to a much higher place of priority. So what can we do as Christians in order to get control of our lives and the use of our time? We can make a decision to subordinate mundane earthly activities to heavenly spiritual ones. In other words, *we can put God first!* This is something all of us are responsible for individually. Just as we are called to **"humble ourselves"** (1 Peter 5:6), so we are responsible to make decisions about the use of our limited time on this earth. During Jesus' earthly ministry we read:

So He Himself *often* withdrew into the wilderness and prayed (Luke 5:16). **He went out to the mountain to pray, and continued all night in prayer to God** (Luke 6:12).

Jesus was willing to do the unconventional in the eyes of the culture in which He lived. I don't think many people at that time made the habit of separating themselves so completely from others in order to pray. And how many would have spent a whole night in prayer then, and how many would do it today? As Christians we should be willing to march to the beat of a different drum from the ordinary lifestyles of others because of the very fact we are called with a high and holy calling. I am not suggesting we should purposely try to be strange or peculiar in the eyes of others, but certainly there should be something spiritually different about us as true disciples and servants of Christ.

What if Jesus had not spent those private times in prayer as recorded in the gospels? Such a scenario is unthinkable to me. How could Jesus ever neglect or forsake those times of communion with His heavenly Father? Prayer was His lifeline to the Father for the strength He needed to fulfill His mission successfully. Do we need any less communion with our Lord in this twenty-first century to know and fulfill God's mission for us as professed followers of Jesus Christ? Prayer is our lifeline to know the Father's will for us just as it was for Jesus. He said,

"I do not seek My own will but the will of the Father who sent Me" (John 5:30). And, **"For I have come down from heaven, not to do My own will, but the will of Him who sent Me"** (John 6:38). And, **"The words that I speak to you I do not speak on My own** *authority;* **but the Father who dwells in Me does the works"** (John 14:10).

Jesus testified and confirmed the truth that even the very words He spoke came to Him with inspiration from His Father. This was made possible because of the continual daily spiritual connection between them. It was obviously Jesus' prayer times alone with the Father that made His words and ministry so powerful.

Do we have a desire for the ministry God has called each one of us to do to be inspired from heaven? How could we want anything less? In other words, do we have such an intimate connection with the Lord and the Holy Spirit that our words and actions in ministry truly represent Him? Prayer is the only foundation for such a possibility. This is why the Apostle Paul wrote, **"Pray without ceasing"** (1 Thessalonians 5:17). And, **"I thank God, whom I serve with a pure conscience, as** *my* **forefathers** *did* **as without ceasing I remember you in my prayers night and day"** (2 Timothy 1:3). How many of us could say this is true of our own prayer lives?

Many years ago I had a vivid dream. In my dream I saw a long railroad train traveling from left to right as it passed rapidly in front of me. On every boxcar in huge bold letters was just one word, PRAY. The message was simply, PRAY, PRAY, PRAY, as I watched each of the passing boxcars on a train that seemingly had no end.

Why would we not pray? Why would we not avail ourselves of such and awesome privilege? Why would we let the hours, days, weeks and months slip by without doing what we know we should be doing? Here's the answer: We have not established our spiritual priorities correctly, and we are letting the influence of the world, the flesh and the devil have sway over our time.

Christians are either in relationship with God through prayer, or in relationship with the world, the flesh and the devil through lack of prayer. We cannot have it both ways! We should be taking definite steps to discipline ourselves for the ministry of prayer. If *we* don't do this, who will? James writes:

"But be doers of the word, and not hearers only, deceiving yourselves. For if anyone is a hearer of the word and not a doer, he is like a man observing his natural face in a mirror; for he observes himself, goes away, and immediately forgets what kind of man he was" (James 1:22-24).

Using James' illustration we can imagine someone looking in a mirror at their reflection, seeing the need to wash their face, and then leaving without doing it. Have we been guilty of this by failing to put into practice the clear instructions given us in the Word of God? I know I have. As an example: In order to write a book like this one I realize the only way it can be completed is by sitting in front of my computer on my desk chair and beginning to type. In other words I need to follow basic procedures to get the job done. But for a book like this my disciplined action of positioning myself physically to write must be preceded by prayer or nothing of eternal value will be accomplished.

The Bible says, **"So teach *us* to number our days, that we may gain a heart of wisdom"** (Psalm 90:12). And, **"Then He spoke a parable to them, that**

men always ought to pray and not lose heart" (Luke 18:1).

Do we want to live through the days of our lives with the wisdom of God? We should not hide our heads in the sand and avoid thinking about the brevity of our earthly lives. As mentioned earlier, each of us has an allotted time on earth that diminishes by each passing minute. We should take seriously the words of Jesus that prayer should be a continual part of our daily lives. Not just any prayer, but prayer that expects God to answer, and prayer that encourages us not to **"lose heart."** Any sincere Christian would love to see revival take place with souls continually being added to the kingdom of God.

George Mueller (1805-1898) was a Christian evangelist in England who by the miraculous supply of God was able to care for over 10,000 orphans by faith. He was one of God's faithful servants who saw amazing answers to his prayers, especially those he prayed for to be saved. When asked about his approach to God in prayer he said:

> "There are five conditions which I always endeavor to fulfill, in observing which I have the assurance of answer to my prayer:
>
> 1. I have not the least doubt because I am assured that it is the Lord's will to save them, for He willeth that all men should be saved and come to the knowledge of the truth (1 Tim. 2:4); and we have the assurance 'that if we ask anything according to his will, he heareth us' (1 John 5:14).
>
> 2. I have never pleaded for their salvation in my own name, but in the blessed name of my

precious Lord Jesus, and on His merits alone (John 1:14).

3. I always firmly believed in the willingness of God to hear my prayers (Mark 11:24).

4. I am not conscious of having yielded to any sin, for 'if I regard iniquity in my heart, the Lord will not hear me' when I call (Ps. 66:18).

5. I have persevered in believing prayer for more than fifty-two years for some, and shall continue till the answer comes: 'Shall not God avenge his own elect which cry day and night unto him?'" (Luke 18:7). (Andrew Murray. *The Prayer Life*. Moody Press, Chicago. 1982 123,124).

Mueller devoted himself to the discipline of prayer and saw by faith the results he was expecting. What use would it be to pray if we do not have faith for the answer? Yet, I have heard prayers which I don't think I would be interested in answering if I myself were God. I'm sure I have also prayed prayers like this in the past. We must become so passionate about prayer that we live in it moment-by-moment with the expectancy for God's gracious response.

Elijah of Old Testament times should be a great encouragement to us as we bring our requests to God. In First Kings 17:1 Elijah said to Ahab king of Israel, **"As the Lord God of Israel lives, before whom I stand, there shall not be dew nor rain these years, except at my word."** How could he be so absolutely confident that his words would be fulfilled? I think the clue is found in the phrase **"before whom I stand."** Elijah had obviously been in close communion and relationship with God to have received such a specific prophetic word. I have heard of pastors praying that it would not rain on

Sunday mornings so people would not stay away because of the weather. But Elijah believed, and God answered his unusual request. James 5:16-18 gives us more insight into Elijah's prayer life. It reads:

"The effective, fervent prayer of a righteous man avails much. Elijah was a man with a nature like ours, and he prayed earnestly that it would not rain; and it did not rain on the land for three years and six months. And he prayed again, and the heaven gave rain."

How earnestly did Elijah pray? He was a perfect example of an illustration Jesus used to teach about effective prayer in Luke 18:1-8:

Then He spoke a parable to them, that men always ought to pray and not lose heart, saying: "There was in a certain city a judge who did not fear God nor regard man. Now there was a widow in that city; and she came to him, saying, 'Get justice for me from my adversary.' And he would not for a while; but afterward he said within himself, 'Though I do not fear God nor regard man, yet because this widow troubles me I will avenge her, lest by her continual coming she weary me.'"

Then the Lord said, "Hear what the unjust judge said. And shall God not avenge His own elect who cry out day and night to Him, though He bears long with them? I tell you that He will avenge them speedily. Nevertheless, when the Son of Man comes, will He really find faith on the earth?"

Simply put, we must really mean it from the depth of our inner being when we pray. Even if God were to say no to our requests or answer in a different way from what we expected, we lose nothing by praying with all the faith and expectancy we have in our hearts? If we realize God always knows best concerning the situation we are praying about, we can safely trust in His providence to answer our prayers in the best possible way. And we always need to remember that His timing is perfect; He is never late! But the point is we must always pray in faith. The two scriptural examples above both emphasize the need for persistent faith.

Elijah had the assurance in his heart that it was God's will to bring the more than three-years-drought to an end. But his faith and faithfulness to God was about to be tested. This can often happen to us today even after we feel assured of God's will in a matter. It may take time for the manifestation of the answer to our prayers. After all, we have an enemy who would hinder our prayers if he could. We can be bold enough to ask God to speed things up, but again, we must remember His timing is always perfect. I have sometimes used scriptural prayers like this one: **"Answer me speedily, O Lord"** (Psalm 143:7). In Elijah's case he had already told King Ahab that rain was coming, but as of yet there was no sign of it in the heavens. So Elijah went to prayer knowing he had committed himself to a quick answer. We read:

And Elijah went up to the top of Carmel; then he bowed down on the ground, and put his face between his knees, and said to his servant, "Go up now, look toward the sea." So he went up and looked, and said, "There is nothing." And seven times he said, "Go again." Then it came to pass the seventh *time,* **that he said, "There is a cloud, as small as a man's hand, rising out of the sea!" ... and there was a heavy rain** (1 Kings 18:42.43.45).

We have probably all heard sermons about this event and how Elijah's servant must have wondered how many more times he would have to go and look for rain. The obvious and simple lesson is that persistence in prayer is required along with faith. Like the woman and the unjust judge in the illustration given by Jesus, we see that persistent faith is what Jesus is looking for. We also see that Jesus challenges all of us with His statement at the end of His illustration, **"Nevertheless, when the Son of Man comes, will He really find faith on the earth?"** Yes, it must always be by the combination of prayer and faith together that God will be pleased to answer and move on our behalf.

In my book *Found Wanting: America Needs Revival Now!* I tell about the persistence of some who prayed for revival in the Hebrides Islands. As told by Duncan Campbell it reads:

> "Now I am sure that you will be interested to know how, in November 1949, this gracious movement began on the island of Lewis. Two old women, one of them 84 years of age and the other 82—one of them stone blind—were really burdened because of the appalling state of their own parish. It was true that not a single young person attended public worship. Not a single young man or young woman went to church. They spent their day perhaps reading or walking, but the church was left out of the picture. And those two women were greatly concerned as they made it a special matter of prayer.
>
> A verse gripped them: **"I will pour water on him that is thirsty and floods upon the dry ground"** (Isaiah 44:3). They were so burdened that both of them decided to spend so much time in prayer twice a week. On Tuesday they got on their knees at 10 o'clock in the evening and remained on their knees until 3 or 4 o'clock in the

morning—two old women in a very humble cottage."

(www.shilohouse.org/Hebrides_Revival.htm. Accessed June 19, 2017).

ABOVE: The two sisters with Duncan Campbell *circa* 1949.

(images.search.yahoo.com/yhs/search?p=hebrides+revival. Accessed June 19, 2017).

Campbell continued by telling how these two elderly sisters called the local minister and challenged him to form a group and pray two nights a week just as they were doing. The minister complied, and soon a group of seven men met a few times a week in a straw-filled barn to seek the Lord for revival. They continued praying in earnest for several months. One night the need for personal holiness was impressed upon them. Psalm 24:3,4 was quoted:

"Who shall ascend into the hill of the LORD? Or who shall stand in his holy place? He that hath clean hands, and a pure heart; who hath not lifted up his soul unto vanity, nor sworn deceitfully" (KJV). After this, one of the young men fell to the floor as he was praying and seemed overcome by the presence of God as if in a trance. Campbell continues:

"When that happened in the barn, the power of God swept into the parish. And an awareness of God gripped the community such as hadn't been known for over 100 years. An awareness of God—that's revival, that's revival. And on the following day, the looms were silent; little work was done on the farms as men and women gave themselves to thinking on eternal things gripped by eternal realities."
(www.shilohouse.org/Hebrides_Revival.htm. Accessed June 19, 2017*).*

It is important that after reading an account like this we do not think we have to come before God with unrelenting persistence until we manage to twist God's arm and force Him to bring revival. God is always ready to bless His people. The question is: Are we ready to be blessed? Do we have an intimate enough relationship with Him so that the Holy Spirit has full access and freedom to flow through our lives with the ministry He alone can provide? We have to come to the place where we are truly committed and surrendered to be true servants of the Lord. It may take time for the Lord to deal with us and get us to the place where we are ready for service. But God can also do a quick work (Rod Butterworth, *Found Wanting: America Needs Revival Now!* 2016 35-37).

America is in dire straits spiritually in this first quarter of the twenty-first-century. We are seeing degeneracy increase in large portions of our population. Christians have the answer if we will only put into actual practice what God's Word tells us to do. God is saying to us "If we pray...," and He is waiting to see what we will do. At the time of this writing (June 2017) we have a new administration in America. The vicious attacks against our new legitimately elected president and administrative leadership are practically unprecedented according to historians. Some have evenly openly suggested that our president should be assassinated!

Our nation is so tragically divided at this time that the words "civil war" are being uttered by some as a possible foreboding of the future. As Christians, surely we can see the connection between spiritual stagnation and the increase of political, social, and moral chaos? Surely we can see the connection between pushing aside the Bible and its standards of moral righteousness as unimportant, and the darkness of human minds completely abandoned to ungodly beliefs and degenerative lifestyles.

Wake up Christians! I speak to myself. And once again I repeat, as I probably will many times throughout this book, that the *only* hope for the future of America is concerted, earnest, passionate, intercessory prayer with a bold approach to God—like Abraham's when he was desperately bargaining for the safety of his nephew Lot. We read:

And Abraham came near and said, "Would You also destroy the righteous with the wicked? Suppose there were fifty righteous within the city; would You also destroy the place and not spare *it* for the fifty righteous that were in it? Far be it from You to do such a thing as this, to slay the righteous with the wicked, so that the righteous should be as the wicked; far be it from You! Shall not the Judge of all the earth do right?"

So the Lord said, "If I find in Sodom fifty righteous within the city, then I will spare all the place for their sakes." (Genesis 18:23-26)

God was about to destroy the city of Sodom and others because of their extreme sexual perversions and wickedness. Abraham was obviously very concerned about the safety of Lot and his family and continued to bargain with God by reducing the number of supposed righteous people down to ten. But there were not even ten righteous people in Sodom and God's judgment was not to be averted.

Areas around the Dead Sea to this day show the remains and physical evidence of God's destruction of these cities through the raining down upon them of fire and brimstone. With this judgment of God in mind I am thankful for the knowledge that there are more than ten righteous believers in America today—in fact, surely millions. But there is also extreme wickedness taking place in our land that will surely lead to future judgment.

As Abraham was concerned for the welfare of his nephew Lot, so we should be concerned not only for our own immediate family, but for all the families of America? Do we petition God passionately for the spiritual renewal this country needs so desperately? Do we really believe that prayer will make any difference? I hope we do. Next, we will look at what it means to seek God's face.

CHAPTER 5

AND SEEK MY FACE

Facial expressions are revealing. Over twenty face muscles make it possible for an amazing array of expressions that reveal the gamut of human emotions. Married people are usually especially sensitive to recognizing the facial messages of their partners and what they mean. The closer the relationship, the more intimate knowledge and understanding of the other is known. So what is God actually saying when He invites us to seek His face?

Interestingly, there are scriptures in the Old Testament giving warnings to the Israelites about getting too close to God. For example, Exodus 33;20 says, **"You cannot see My face; for no man shall see Me, and live."** And when the people of Israel reached Mt. Sinai they experienced an awesome revelation of God's presence as recorded in Exodus 20:18 which reads:

Now all the people witnessed the thunderings, the lightning flashes, the sound of the trumpet, and the mountain smoking; and when the people saw *it*, they trembled and stood afar off. In Exodus 19:21 it says, **And the LORD said to Moses, "Go down and warn the people, lest they break through to gaze at the LORD, and many of them perish."**

There was one person, however, who was privileged to have a face-to-face encounter with God, and that was Moses. However, this does not mean Moses saw a literal face of God, but experienced such a close relationship with Him when meeting with Him in the Holy Place of the tabernacle, that his face reflected some of the brilliance of God's presence. A special relationship had developed between Moses and God beginning with the incident of the burning bush. This unusual relationship continued for the length of Moses' life, and in this sense it separated him from the ordinary Israelites. This unique relationship is also clearly seen after God instructed Moses to build the tabernacle or tent of meeting in the wilderness. In Exodus 33:10-12 we read:

All the people saw the pillar of cloud standing *at* the tabernacle door, and all the people rose and worshiped, each man *in* his tent door. So the LORD spoke to Moses face to face, as a man speaks to his friend. And he would return to the camp, but his servant Joshua the son of Nun, a young man, did not depart from the tabernacle [there is no indication that Joshua entered the special area of the tabernacle called the Holy Place where the presence of God dwelt, although from this time on he also had a special relationship with God].

In Exodus 34:29-35 we see something supernatural happened to Moses after his close one-on-one encounters with God:

Now it was so, when Moses came down from Mount Sinai (and the two tablets of the Testimony *were* in Moses' hand when he came down from the mountain), that Moses did not know that the skin of his face shone while he talked with Him.

So when Aaron and all the children of Israel saw Moses, behold, the skin of his face shone, and they were afraid to come near him. Then Moses called to them, and Aaron and all the rulers of the congregation returned to him; and Moses talked with them. Afterward all the children of Israel came near, and he gave them as commandments all that the LORD had spoken with him on Mount Sinai.

And when Moses had finished speaking with them, he put a veil on his face. But whenever Moses went in before the LORD to speak with Him, he would take the veil off until he came out; and he would come out and speak to the children of Israel whatever he had been commanded. And whenever the children of Israel saw the face of Moses, that the skin of Moses' face shone, then Moses would put the veil on his face again, until he went in to speak with Him.

In Genesis 1:3 God said, "Let there be light"; and there was light. And the Apostle John wrote, "This is the message which we have heard from Him and declare to you, that God is light and in Him is no darkness at all" (1 John 1:5). No wonder then, that after spending intimate face-to-face meetings with the God of light, Moses' face shone with such holy radiance. In fact, this was such an evidence of the supernatural to the ordinary Israelite it produced fear in their hearts. "So when Aaron and all the children of Israel saw Moses, behold, the skin of his face shone, and they were afraid to come near him" (Exodus 34:30).

Nevertheless, the Bible strongly encourages the godly to seek the face of the Lord. We are to desire such close intimacy with the Lord in order to reflect His light to those around us. First Chronicles 16:11 says, "Seek the Lord and His strength; Seek His face evermore." Psalm 27:8 reads, *"When You said,* "Seek My face," My heart said to You, Your face, Lord, I will seek."

Here is the message I understand from all of this: God has already sought us and desires this close relationship with us through Jesus, now it is our responsibility to seek Him for the fullness of His power and the living out in our daily lives of His purpose for us.

He is inviting us into this secret place of communion with Him to bless us in every part of our lives. If we can be honest and transparent enough to come to the Lord without ulterior motives of self-exaltation, and humble ourselves before Him, we can experience the workings of God in and through our lives in almost unbelievable ways. As we earnestly seek Him we will see definite answers to prayer that in the natural would seem impossible. Jesus said,

"But seek first the kingdom of God and His righteousness, and all these things shall be added to you" (Matthew 6:33).

We need to put the spotlight of truth upon ourselves and see if our desires match up to these words of Jesus. On what do we spend most of our time and energy on a daily basis? Jesus came with a definite purpose in mind which was **"to seek and to save that which was lost"** (Luke 19:10).

Are we sharing the same desires as our Lord for the eternal destiny of those around us? Do we pray regularly for the salvation of relatives or friends who are lost? When God speaks of seeking His face there has to be a reason and specific needs for which we are seeking Him. If we seem to have no urgent needs it is surely an indication we are not in a close enough relationship with Him to know His heart. It comes down to whether or not we have the right desires, which we will have if God has enlightened us with His desires. Do we have the heart of God with concern for the most important things in life and apply ourselves with prayerful passion and devotion toward these ends?

Over 500 years before Christ when Daniel realized the time had come for God's people to be delivered from Babylon and return to Jerusalem we read, **"Then I set my face toward the Lord God to make**

request by prayer and supplications, with fasting, sackcloth, and ashes" (Daniel 9:3). We can see that Daniel wanted God to see the earnestness and sincerity in his face as he began to seek God.

One way Christians can express their seriousness in seeking God is by praying with fasting as Daniel did. He prayed a powerful prayer in confessing the sins of his people, and just before he received amazing revelations from God about the future we read,

"In those days, I, Daniel, was mourning three full weeks. I ate no pleasant food, no meat or wine came into my mouth, nor did I anoint myself at all, till three whole weeks were fulfilled" (Daniel 10:2,3).

When we observe the unprecedented ungodly attacks against America from the powers of darkness in this twenty-first century we should be weeping before God for deliverance and restoration like Daniel. Fasting combined with earnest prayer will give evidence of our heart's sincerity.

I believe God is greatly concerned about the future of America because the Judeo-Christian values upon which it was uniquely founded are under severe attack. If we are not concerned, we are not on the same wavelength as God.

If we, as Christians, don't want to hear about the degenerative forces which are at work to destroy America, but tend to hide our heads in the sands of indifference hoping to continue undisturbed in our own little selfish self-centered worlds, I'm afraid we will be unavoidably shocked beyond belief in the days ahead. If God is concerned, we had better be concerned. Not only concerned, but actively applying the solution God puts before us if we will only obey His Word and His leading.

In other words, seek the One, the only One who can bring restoration and revival. Otherwise, the other word in the title of this book will become a reality—*rejection!*

Yes, prayer with fasting is a powerful way to seek God as long as it is done with all sincerity and purity of motive. There is something about depriving the body of food for a while that has a humbling effect on the heart. In my book *Found Wanting: America Needs Revival Now!* I wrote the following:

> Some churches start each New Year with a planned period of fasting and prayer for the Lord's blessing. Fasting, meaning abstaining from food, can be a valuable means of insight, support and encouragement during times of seeking God in prayer. This is something that many professed Christians rarely, if ever, refer to as a beneficial practice for believers. However, it has been practiced by individuals and groups from the very beginning of the New Testament Church, as well as extending back into Old Testament times.
>
> Those who have experienced as least short periods of fasting for two or three days or more while earnestly seeking the Lord, know that such a spiritual exercise can have a beneficial humbling effect. It can provide new and deeper insight into how God sees us and how we see ourselves.
>
> In a few words, this is the value of fasting, not to twist God's arm into meeting our perceived needs or desires, but to position ourselves before God in all humility in order that He can begin to minister to us and reveal more of His purposes and plans for us. Matthew 17:21 mentioned above contains the words of Jesus explaining to His disciples why they were unsuccessful in delivering a boy from demonic affliction. He said,

"However, this kind does not go out except by prayer and fasting."

The disciples had delivered others from demon spirits before with apparent ease, but this time they were unable to do so. How can prayer and fasting combined together help in difficult cases like the situation facing the disciples? It can get us more in line with God's motives and purposes so that we can be as spiritual lightning rods for the flow and energy of the Holy Spirit through us.

We must always remember that it is His power that brings the victory, not anything arising from our natural selves. There is considerable information available on this subject of fasting through books and the Internet, and I would suggest a careful study before embarking on an actual fast. There are precautions that would be wise to consider regarding personal health issues, but in general, fasting from food (but not water) for the average person and for periods up to five or six days should not be of great concern. More comprehensive knowledge of fasting would need to be understood if longer periods of fasting are being considered.

It is true that other religions practice fasting in a variety of ways, but would be of no spiritual value unless directed with the right motives to the one true God. Most people who have fasted for at least several days testify to an increased sensitivity to spiritual things. It is important for the Christian to have the right motives when fasting, and to give the Word of God continual attention through reading and meditation. I love Psalm 1 which doesn't talk directly about the subject of fasting, but tells us what our motives and attitude should be as we seek God. A portion of it reads:

"But his delight *is* **in the law of the Lord, and in His law he meditates day and night. He shall be like a tree planted by the rivers of water, that brings forth its fruit in its season, whose leaf also shall not wither; and whatever he does shall prosper"** (Psalm 1:2,3).

Our desire should always focus on our lives being more fruitful for the kingdom of God. Sincerely seeking God with fasting and prayer should indicate our willingness to submit to His will for our lives in all things. The results can be extremely rewarding and profitable both for ourselves and those around us. Here is a partial list of Scriptures that speak of fasting:

Judges 20:26. Then all the children of Israel, that is, all the people, went up and came to the house of God and wept. They sat there before the LORD and **fasted** that day until evening; and they offered burnt offerings and peace offerings before the LORD.

1 Samuel 7:6. So they gathered together at Mizpah, drew water, and poured it out before the Lord. And they **fasted** that day, and said there, "We have sinned against the Lord."

1 Samuel 31:13. Then they took their bones and buried them under the tamarisk tree at Jabesh, and **fasted** seven days.

2 Samuel 12:16. David therefore pleaded with God for the child, and David **fasted** and went in and lay all night on the ground.

1 Chronicles 10:12. All the valiant men arose and took the body of Saul and the bodies of his sons; and they brought them to Jabesh, and buried their bones under the tamarisk tree at Jabesh, and **fasted** seven days.

Ezra 8:21. Then I proclaimed a **fast** there at the river of Ahava, that we might humble ourselves before our God, to seek from Him the right way for us and our little ones and all our possessions.

Nehemiah 1:4. So it was, when I heard these words, that I sat down and wept, and mourned for many days; I was **fasting and praying** before the God of heaven.

Esther 4:16. "Go, gather all the Jews who are present in Shushan, and **fast** for me; neither eat nor drink for three days, night or day. My maids and I will **fast** likewise. And so I will go to the king, which is against the law; and if I perish, I perish!"

Psalm 35:13. I humbled myself with **fasting**.

Isaiah 58:6. "Is this not the **fast** that I have chosen: to loose the bonds of wickedness, to undo the heavy burdens, to let the oppressed go free, and that you break every yoke?

Jeremiah 36:9. In the ninth month, that they proclaimed a **fast** before the LORD to all the people in Jerusalem, and to all the people who came from the cities of Judah to Jerusalem.

Daniel 9:3. Then I set my face toward the Lord God to make request by prayer and supplications, with **fasting**, sackcloth, and ashes.

Joel 2:12. "Now, therefore," says the LORD, "Turn to Me with all your heart, with **fasting**, with weeping, and with mourning."

Jonah 3:5. So the people of Nineveh believed God, proclaimed a **fast**, and put on sackcloth, from the greatest to the least of them.

Zechariah 7:5. "Say to all the people of the land, and to the priests: 'When you **fasted** and mourned in the fifth and seventh months during those seventy years, did you really **fast** for Me—for Me?

Matthew 4:2. And when He had **fasted** forty days and forty nights, afterward He was hungry.

Matthew 6:16-18. "Moreover, when you **fast**, do not be like the hypocrites, with a sad countenance. For they disfigure their faces that they may appear to men to be fasting. Assuredly, I say to you, they have their reward. But you, when you **fast**, anoint your head and wash your face, so that you do not appear to men to be **fasting**, but to your Father who is in the secret place; and your Father who sees in secret will reward you openly.

Matthew 17:21. "However, this kind does not go out except by prayer and **fasting**."

Luke 2:37. And this woman was a widow of about eighty-four years, who did not depart from the temple, but served God with **fastings and prayers** night and day.

Acts 13:2. As they ministered to the Lord and **fasted**, the Holy Spirit said, "Now separate to Me Barnabas and Saul for the work to which I have called them."

Acts 14:23. So when they had appointed elders in every church, and prayed with **fasting**, they commended them to the Lord in whom they had believed.

1 Corinthians 7:5. Do not deprive one another

except with consent for a time, that you may give yourselves to **fasting and prayer**; and come together again so that Satan does not tempt you because of your lack of self-control.

2 Corinthians 11:26,27. In perils among false brethren; in weariness and toil, in sleeplessness often, in hunger and thirst, in **fastings** often. ((Rod Butterworth. *Found Wanting: America Needs Revival Now!* 2016 229-233).

In the verse quoted above from Matthew 6:17,18 Jesus included a promise for those who fast with the right motives. He said,

"But you, when you fast, anoint your head and wash your face, so that you do not appear to men to be fasting, but to your Father who is in the secret place; and your Father who sees in secret will reward you openly" (KJV).

The Father notices us when we seek Him for the right purposes (of course, the Father knows everything about everyone all the time). In fact, as He sees what we are doing for Him by seeking benefit and advancement for the kingdom of God, He has promised to reward us. Would it not be a reward to see millions of America's ungodly find the true meaning of life through Jesus Christ? Would it be worth seeking God for an amazing demonstration of the power of the Holy Spirit to see righteousness prevail in our country? The way ahead is to simply do what God's Word tells us to do—to seek Him with all of our hearts.

There is a wonderful scripture which should challenge all of us to continually seek the Lord. The Apostle Paul wrote:

"But we all, with unveiled face, beholding as in a mirror the glory of the Lord, are being

transformed into the same image from glory to glory, just as by the Spirit of the Lord" (2 Corinthians 3:18).

The unsaved world needs to see revived Christians. This is the biblical way God has ordained for His truth and the Gospel to be proclaimed to the lost world. In fact, Jesus prayed in John 17:21, **"That they all may be one, as You, Father, *are* in Me, and I in You; that they also may be one in Us, that the world may believe that You sent Me."** Yes, if we have that *unveiled-face* relationship with the Lord, we, as the body of Christ will demonstrate such amazing unity that its affect upon the world will be to lead them to Jesus.

Yet, what disunity we see in the body of Christ. All true believers who by faith in Christ's sacrificial death have been forgiven of their sins are part of His spiritual body. Did not such lack of unity cause Jesus to weep for Jerusalem? It was because of the disunity of those who confidently claimed a relationship with God, but had none that He weeped. The self-righteous Pharisees were deceived in their spiritual blindness.

Personally, if I find myself considering other professed Christians inferior because they do not believe doctrinally exactly the same as the denominational beliefs I happen to espouse, I cannot have the heart of Jesus! I should be weeping, praying and fasting for God's people to be revived in love and unity for the sake of the kingdom of God. This is what the ungodly in America need to see—the power of God's love demonstrated through a united body of believers. If we can see ourselves the way God sees us in our disunity as believers in America, we may well feel like Ezra who prayed,

"O my God, I am too ashamed and humiliated to lift up my face to You, my God; for our iniquities have risen higher than *our* heads,

and our guilt has grown up to the heavens (Ezra 9:6).

Yet, in spite of our **"iniquities"** as a nation, our gracious Lord invites us to come before Him with our petitions. We can pray as the Psalmist,

"Do not hide Your face from me in the day of my trouble; Incline Your ear to me; In the day that I call, answer me speedily" (Psalm 102:2).

Yes, America is in trouble in these early days of the twenty-first century. The only answer that will be of lasting eternal value is to seek His face with all of our hearts. Let us pray,

"God be merciful to us and bless us, *And* cause His face to shine upon us" (Psalm 67:1).

CHAPTER 6

AND TURN FROM THEIR WICKED WAYS

"Thou shalt have no other gods before me" (Exodus 20:3 KJV). Idols, idols, everywhere! America has an abundance of evil idols that need to be exposed, confessed and destroyed! Idolatry has even invaded the Church! We make heroes of people in entertainment and sports who should not be lifted up and idolized. There must be a turning away from these sinful distractions with the help of the Holy Spirit if there is to be hope for an America that is more righteous than unrighteous. Recognition of our true unrighteous spiritual state before God must be recognized, confessed, and repented of in all sincerity. We must come before God in humble obedience, rededication and commitment if we are to be His true servants. Donald C. Stamps writes:

> "The practice of self-examination, humility and turning from sin within the church is necessary if the church is to see any degree of spiritual revival among believers and any significant influence for Christ in their communities" (Donald C. Stamps. *Fire Bible: Modern English Version* Life Publishers International, 2015 Notes 1862).

I reiterate once more the solemn reality that America finds itself in a desperate situation spiritually in these early days of the twenty-first century. Our country hangs in the balance of either continuing a downward spiral into more degeneracy, debauchery, violence, social unrest and unrighteous ungodly lifestyles, or into possible change for the better through Christians who take advantage of the spiritual weapons God is willing to exercise through us if we will only seek Him in all earnestness.

When I look at the American Church as a whole I have to ask: Where are the Christians who will enter the spiritual warfare with holy zeal and self-sacrifice of time and effort to engage the enemy and gain victories for the kingdom of God? As professed Christians we truly need a new revelation of how God sees us as individuals and how He sees us as the body of Christ in the American Church. Such may be a devastating revelation of our true state causing us to weep many tears of sorrow before Him. But such an honest reaction as this would surely point to the possibility of a good beginning leading to change for better things. We must be willing to let God deal with us according to His knowledge of our needs, and if we do this we can have vision, hope, and expectation for a more spiritual and godly future for our nation.

Can Christians be deceived into thinking they have no personal idols or wicked ways in the eyes of the Lord? Absolutely! In fact, if I am deceived I will not realize I am deceived while in that state. This is a scary thought for Christians to consider. I certainly don't want to be deceived, and no normal person, especially a Christian, would want to be unaware of such a personal undesirable condition.

Think of Eve in the Garden of Eden. She was in a perfect environment with every need met, knew God personally, and was well aware of the conditions God had given for continued blessing. But she was deceived by Satan's smooth talk that seemed so authoritative and sensible. He cunningly seduced her with overtures of slick persuasion that appealed to her natural desires and ego. Today, in like manner, it is possible for professed Christians to think they are pleasing God, when in reality they may discover the life God has planned for them is quite different from the way they have been living. I can testify to times in my past when I thought I was pleasing to God, but when I became sincere about coming before God and seeking Him for direction, I found to my shock and shame that I was far from where God wanted me to be as His servant.

Yes, when God turns His searchlight of truth upon us it is transparently revealing and will definitely help us keep humble before Him. I hope all Christians will agree with me that we need the discipline and chastisement of the Lord at times to help keep us faithful and fruitful in our relationship with Him. The Bible tells us,

"My son, do not despise the chastening of the Lord, nor be discouraged when you are rebuked by Him; for whom the Lord loves He chastens, and scourges every son whom He receives" (Hebrews 12:5,6).

Our key scripture tells us we need to *turn* from our wicked ways. When we discover the things God is not pleased with in our lives the responsibility rests with us to instigate change. Ezekiel 14:6 reads, **"Thus says the Lord GOD: 'Repent, turn away from your idols, and turn your faces away from all your abominations.'"** In Ezekiel's day many of the Israelites had set up literal idols in their homes, and were involved in practices such as magic arts and divination which are an abomination to God.

Americans have idols in their homes today of a different kind than the Israelites of old. There are altars in front of wide-screen TVs, and smart phones and video games wasting countless hours of unprofitable couch-potato sedentary activities. Many live to eat and drink their favorite unhealthy delicacies and die at a young age instead of eating healthily to live with intentional purpose. In other words, people live for temporary pleasures and self-centeredness rather than for a worthwhile purpose with eternal values in mind. We can all be caught up in some exhilarating moment of excitement of things that have no lasting value in light of eternity.

People tend to put out of their minds the fact that one day they will die and have to face the consequences of their choices and the way they have lived their lives. But can all these things really apply to Christians? Unfortunately, yes. I should say to *professed Christians* because the above descriptions should not apply to a devoted follower of Jesus Christ.

When the Lord tells His people to **"turn from their wicked ways"** He is giving an opportunity by His grace for the guilty ones to get back on track with Him with an intimate personal relationship. This may well put such individuals in conflict with family and friends who do not see the need to be so spiritually radical as to change lifestyles by cutting out activities they have not yet realized are harmful to their own future. It will take courage and determination to make the necessary changes, but it will reap great rewards in the future.

Where is the root of our evil ways? Surface clean-up will not suffice. It has to be a heart change at the very foundation of our beings for a true turning from any wickedness within us. The Apostle Paul wrote these words to Christians in the Corinthian Church,

"Therefore, having these promises, beloved, let us cleanse ourselves from all filthiness of the flesh and spirit, perfecting holiness in the fear of the Lord" (2 Corinthians 7:1).

Let me repeat; Paul wrote these words to *Christians!* Notice the words, **"flesh and spirit"** which refer to a combination and cleansing of both the outward man and the inner spiritual man. In other words, we could say there has to be a *clean sweep* of our total beings in order to be pure vessels of honor before the Lord. There is no other way to be fruitful for the kingdom of God.

Notice also the phrase **"the fear of the Lord."** Some ministers of the Gospel may be criticized with the complaint that their preaching about eternal destinies is making people afraid. But this is not a bad thing. I grew up with a friend who openly confessed that as a teenager he became a Christian because he was afraid of going to hell. After serving in the military he entered the ministry and served the Lord faithfully for the rest of his life.

Yes, we should always have a healthy reverential fear of the Lord. After all, we are His creation, and as such we should give Him the respect and honor due Him. If we become aware of our failings before the Lord as He reveals them to us, in holy reverence we should repent and accept the grace of His forgiveness in order to continue our journey of faith.

Jesus reminded those He taught of the importance of keeping the first and greatest commandment of all; **"You shall love the Lord your God with all your heart, with all your soul, and with all your mind"** (Matthew 22:37). In other words, as said above, we are to love God with our whole beings. But if we should hold back some unholy affection in the recesses of our hearts we risk the very real danger of the Lord not hearing our prayers—not to mention that an intimate relationship with the Lord will be lacking.

The Bible says, **"If I regard iniquity in my heart, the Lord will not hear *me*"** (Psalm 66:18 KJV). And Jesus reminded us of the need to recognize the root of any wickedness in us when He said, **"But those things which proceed out of the mouth come from** the heart, and they defile a man. For out of the heart proceed evil thoughts, murders, adulteries, fornications, thefts, false witness, blasphemies"** (Matthew 15:18,19).

What a tragedy it is if we profess Christianity, attend church, support the work of God with our giving, say the right words, and appear outwardly to be examples of true Christ-followers, but Jesus would have to say to us, **"These people draw near to Me with their mouth, and honor Me with *their* lips, but their heart is far from Me"** (Matthew 15:8). Once again, we can see the possibility of deception in our hearts. Satan is the master deceiver, and if we just open the door a little way he will whisper to us that everything is fine, even though in God's sight it is not. The Bible reminds us through Jeremiah the prophet,

"The heart *is* deceitful above all *things*, and desperately wicked; who can know it? I, the Lord, search the heart, *I* test the mind, even to give every man according to his ways, according to the fruit of his doings" (Jeremiah 17:9,10).

Jeremiah reminds us that every person reaps what they sow. Since the natural heart cannot be trusted it is of vital importance that we, as Christians, come to the place where we are totally transparent before the Lord. This is the only way to be able to see what things need to be changed in our lives. It is the only way to see the deception of wickedness in ourselves and understand clearly the ungodly things we need to turn away from.

For example, some might think that since involvement in activities such as sports is not in itself wrong, *wicked* may be too strong a term to use. But if there is conviction because of over involvement and time spent, there should be a willingness to make the necessary adjustments. So the truth is that if anything hinders our relationship with God and His purposes for our lives it can be looked upon as wicked. Satan is wicked, and he will certainly exert his influence of deception upon us in any way he can. This is why we need the searchlight of God's holiness to examine our hearts in order to reveal where we stand with Him. Like Daniel we need to pray,

"O Lord, to us *belongs* shame of face, to our kings, our princes, and our fathers, because we have sinned against You" (Daniel 9:8).

What can we expect if we neglect or refuse to come before God with a transparent humble attitude of repentance? Such a course will result in unbelievable shame and remorse in the future, even if we are able to be among those who are privileged to participate in the marriage supper of the Lamb. There will be regrets, and there will be degrees of rewards given by a totally righteous and impartial God.

When dealing with the disobedient people of Israel God showed His love through the warnings He gave them. He said,

"Behold, I *am* against you," says the LORD of hosts; "I will lift your skirts over your face, I will show the nations your nakedness, and the kingdoms your shame" (Nahum 3:5).

Yes, if we are not willing to humble ourselves before God and turn from our wicked ways we will eventually be exposed for who we really are.

Here is the good news: If I simply obey God's urging to turn from my wicked ways in order for my life and testimony to be fruitful for the Gospel and the kingdom of God, I will experience the kind of peace, blessing and fulfillment that only the Lord can give. The Apostle James reminds us, **"Draw near to God and He will draw near to you"** (James 4:8).

Do you want Him to be near you? You know what to do. "**For the L**ORD **your God** *is* **gracious and merciful, and will not turn** *His* **face from you if you return to Him.**" (2 Chronicles 30:9) Let's *turn away from* in order to *turn toward Him!*

CHAPTER 7

THEN I WILL HEAR FROM HEAVEN

Do we *really* believe it? Do we believe in our heart of hearts the many promises in the Bible telling us God hears and answers our prayers? Most people did not expect the things which have recently developed in America as I write this in July 2017. We have a new president and vice-president who openly profess to believe in God and have expressed their appreciation for those who pray for them. President Trump has even said publicly, "Our republic was formed on the basis that freedom is not a gift from government, but that freedom is a gift from God" (National Prayer Breakfast, Washington DC, February 2, 2017). And remarkably for a sitting president to be so transparent and forthright he also said, "In America we don't worship government, we worship God!" (Celebrate Freedom Concert, Washington DC, July 1, 2017). He has also been reported as saying that the five words he likes to hear more than anything else from others are: I am praying for you.

Some are suggesting that God is giving America an extended opportunity to turn from their wicked ways as recounted in the previous chapter. If this is true, we, as Christians, should be actively engaging in the one thing above all others which can change our nation for the better—prayer to the God who hears and answers. Having godly politicians and government leaders is a good thing, but not the answer to the millions of Americans who are walking and living in spiritual darkness without a relationship with God. We need to remember that as far as we can tell from information available, the majority of politicians in Washington are not godly or righteous, and we should be burdened to pray for good changes in our leadership. It is prayer that lays the foundation and inspires action to take back what the enemy has stolen. Abraham Lincoln faced a critical time in his life during the 1860s such as most of us will never have to face. He wrote the following transparent evaluation of America's problems, and pointed to what he believed to be the solution if only people would do it:

> "We have been the recipients of the choicest bounties of Heaven. We have been preserved, these many years, in peace and prosperity. We have grown in numbers, wealth, and power as no other nation has ever grown; but we have forgotten God.
>
> We have forgotten the gracious hand, which preserved us in peace, and multiplied and enriched and strengthened us; and we have vainly imagined, in the deceitfulness of our hearts, that all these blessings were produced by some superior wisdom and virtue of our own. Intoxicated with unbroken success, we have become too self-sufficient . . . too proud to pray to the God that made us" (Roy Basler, ed., *The Collected Works of Abraham Lincoln,* vol. 6, 1862-1863. New Brunswick, N.J.: Rutgers University Press, 1953, 155-57).

Lincoln believed the underlying problem of America was that the people had forgotten to pray. He obviously had faith that if the people prayed there would be good that would ensue from the hand of God. What is to be required of us as Christians today in order to believe that God truly hears and answers our prayers? Faith! Pure unadulterated faith. God is a God of faith. He created the universe and all things existing in perfect faith by the power of His Word. It is a worthless endeavor to pray without active faith. The Apostle James describes this in down-to-earth terms when he wrote about asking God for something specific in prayer—in this case, wisdom:

"If any of you lacks wisdom, let him ask of God, who gives to all liberally and without reproach, and it will be given to him. But let him ask in faith, with no doubting, for he who doubts is like a wave of the sea driven and tossed by the wind. For let not that man suppose that he will receive anything from the Lord; *he is* **a double-minded man, unstable in all his ways"** (James 1:5-8).

Obviously, if we are asking for something we may think is of smaller concern such as wisdom for help when taking a test in school, we may think it easier to have faith for the answer. But if, in our minds, we are asking for something big such as the transformation of millions of people in a nation such as America, we may find it difficult not to have nagging doubts about the possible outcome.

So how do we get to the position of heart and mind belief without doubting. We don't want to be *double-minded*—asking with a vacillating faith moving in and out like the tides of the ocean going back and forth. James doesn't give us any leeway when he writes we should ask, **"with no doubting."** This is surely something we have all struggled with including myself. I believe the foundation of the answer to wavering faith is to be found in our understanding of the will of God. If we can arrive at the knowledge of what the will of God is in the situations we are praying about, it will surely give us courage to ask in faith without doubting. This leads us to another important scripture written by our beloved Apostle John who certainly knew how to pray prayers that God answers. He wrote:

"Now this is the confidence that we have in Him, that if we ask anything according to His will, He hears us. And if we know that He hears us, whatever we ask, we know that we have the petitions that we have asked of Him" (1 John 5:14,15).

Careful consideration of these inspired words of John will give us insight into how to pray in faith without doubting. If it is God's will for something and we know it, wouldn't such knowledge inspire us with great zeal as we pray knowing that the answer was assured? I turn to Norman Grubb—a British Christian missionary, writer and teacher—for the exciting discovery he made concerning assurance that our prayers would be answered. He wrote:

> "To us it is now said that "it is God that worketh in you both to will and to do of His good pleasure." Here lies the secret. The life in Christ is not to be regarded as a life lived by jerks, sometimes in and sometimes out of His will. That is exactly the esoteric view of God which remains with us as grave clothes from the Fall—that God is merely outside us, transcendent, and His will must be interpreted to us by a constant process of revelations, infusions, breakings forth of light into the midst of a normal experience of darkness.
>
> God is transcendent, but, such is the glorious paradox of faith, He is also immanent [near and within]. Gradually we must come familiar with the esoteric truth, Christ in you, joined to the Lord in one spirit, God dwelling in us and walking in us: "The anointing which ye have received of Him abideth in you"; "It is God that worketh in you to will"; and God's guidance must be seen more in

the daily direction of our wills and desires than in sudden words and inspirations.

We must dare to believe that our wills and desires are His, God working them in us, unless we are definitely conscious that they are opposed to Him" (Norman Grubb. *The Law of Faith*. Christian Literature Crusade, Washington, PA 1977 127).

What Grubb is basically saying here is that because of the reality of God's workings *within us* we should expect to sense His will through our conscious mind and desires. Notice Grubb's revealing words, **"We must dare to believe that our wills and desires are His, God working them in us."** But is it not easy to think our thoughts are ours and not God's? And this is a definite possibility which points to the fact that we need to stay close to the Lord in order to have the necessary discernment.

However, if the Word of God agrees with what we are asking for, and we do not sense a lack of peace in our innermost being, then we can go ahead with our petitions and prayers in faith. If God should say no to our request we should accept His response and know it must be for a good reason.

A well-loved scripture which should encourage us with this bold approach to pray in faith without doubting is Psalm 37:4 which reads: **"Delight yourself also in the Lord, and He shall give you the desires of your heart."** Here we see both the condition and the promise laid out before us. How do we *delight in the Lord*? It is by living in that close daily transparent and intimate relationship with Him. Then we can rest our faith on **"He shall give you."** But the secret is found in delighting ourselves in the Lord until His desires are transmuted into our desires. Then we will be encouraged to pray with the kind of faith God is looking for and desiring to see in us. Now look at 1 John 5:14,15 once more:

"Now this is the confidence that we have in Him, that if we ask anything according to His will, He hears us. And if we know that He hears us, whatever we ask, we know that we have the petitions that we have asked of Him"

Notice the unquestioned confidence John exudes when he writes **"we know that we have."** We can think of these powerful words of Scripture as an orderly process: asking—praying His will—He hears—we know we have. If we really grasp this truth it will revolutionize our prayer lives. It will both embolden us and strengthen our determination never to let go of the petitions we believe are according to His will. Yes, God is only too willing to hear our prayers if we determine to position ourselves before Him in willing surrender and exercise the faith He has given us. It is the prayer of faith that gets the ear of God. Have you ever noticed in the gospels that the only time Jesus enthusiastically commended someone was when they exercised faith? One of the greatest examples of this is in Matthew 8:5-10 which reads:

Now when Jesus had entered Capernaum, a centurion came to Him, pleading with Him [his request], **saying, "Lord, my servant is lying at home paralyzed, dreadfully tormented." And Jesus said to him** [Jesus' response revealing His will], **"I will come and heal him."**

The centurion answered and said, "Lord, I am not worthy that You should come under my roof. But only speak a word, and my servant will be healed [he had assurance of the answer]. **For I also am a man under authority, having soldiers under me. And I say to this** *one* **'Go,' and he goes; and to**

another, 'Come,' and he comes; and to my servant, 'Do this,' and he does it."

When Jesus heard it, He marveled, and said to those who followed, "Assuredly, I say to you, I have not found such great faith, not even in Israel!"

Jesus heard the centurion's request and responded favorably. It is obvious from the Gospels that it was the will of God for Jesus to heal the sick at every opportunity He had, that is, providing faith was present or was generated by the words and actions of Jesus. On one occasion when Jesus returned to His hometown of Nazareth we read, **"Now He did not do many mighty works there because of their unbelief"** (Matthew 13:58). Does Jesus and the Father hear our prayer petitions today just as much as this centurion's? Of course! The Book of Psalms is full of encouraging words confirming that God hears our prayers:

"I cried to the LORD with my voice, And He heard me from His holy hill" Selah (Psalm 3:4)

"Hear me when I call, O God of my righteousness! You have relieved me in *my* distress; Have mercy on me, and hear my prayer" (Psalm 4:1).

"But know that the LORD has set apart for Himself him who is godly; The LORD will hear when I call to Him (Psalm 4:3).

"Depart from me, all you workers of iniquity; For the LORD has heard the voice of my weeping" (Psalm 6:8).

"The LORD has heard my supplication; The LORD will receive my prayer" (Psalm 6:9).

"I have called up You, for You will hear me,

O God; Incline Your ear to me, *and* hear my speech" (Psalm 17:6).

"Blessed *be* the LORD, because He has heard the voice of my supplications" (Psalm 28:6).

"For I said in my haste, "I am cut off from before Your eyes"; Nevertheless You heard the voice of my supplications When I cried out to You" (Psalm 31:22).

"I sought the LORD, and He heard me, and delivered me from all my fears" (Psalm 34:4).

"The righteous cry out, and the LORD hears, and delivers them out of all their troubles" (Psalm 34:17).

"For in You, O LORD, I hope; You will hear, O Lord my God" (Psalm 38:15).

"I waited patiently for the LORD; and He inclined to me, and heard my cry" (Psalm 40:1).

"Evening and morning and at noon I will pray, and cry aloud, and He shall hear my voice" (Psalm 55:17).

"For You, O God, have heard my vows; You have given *me* the heritage of those who fear Your name" (Psalm 61:5).

"O You who hear prayer, to You all flesh will come" (Psalm 65:2).

"If I regard iniquity in my heart, the Lord will not hear, b*ut* certainly God has heard *me;* He has attended to the voice of my prayer" (Psalm 66:18,19).

"For the LORD hears the poor, and does not despise His prisoners" (Psalm 69:33).

"In my distress I cried to the LORD, and He heard me" (Psalm 120:1).

"He will fulfill the desire of those who fear Him; He also will hear their cry and save them" (Psalm 145:19).

If we truly have a personal relationship with God and commune with Him in reverential fear with a humble spirit, we should have absolute confidence that our prayers are heard by God. In our key verse from 2 Chronicles 7:14 God says **"I will hear from heaven."** When we engage in effective prayer we are crossing over from our limited earthly dimension into the unlimited heavenly spiritual dimension. Our words are penetrating the heavenly realm into the very holy presence of the God of all creation, which is from where the answers to our prayers are decreed.

The writer of the Book of Hebrews puts it this way when reminding us of the purpose of the Old Testament Tabernacle or Tent of Meeting. It was there where Moses communed with God's presence in the area called the Holiest Place by the Ark of the Covenant. During that time period God chose to manifest His presence above the ark and converse with Moses:

"Therefore, brethren, having boldness to enter the Holiest by the blood of Jesus, by a new and living way which He consecrated for us, through the veil, that is, His flesh, and *having* a High Priest over the house of God, let us draw near with a true heart in full assurance of faith, having our hearts sprinkled from an evil conscience and our bodies washed with pure water.

Let us hold fast the confession of *our* hope without wavering, for He who promised is faithful" (Hebrews 10:19-23).

Yes, our prayers are heard in the holy place of God's presence when we offer them passionately from a sincere heart. Something we need to realize is that even though the answer to our request has been granted by God it may take time for the materialization or manifestation of our prayers to be seen and experienced in reality. This is what Daniel experienced in Old Testament times:

And he [the angel] **said to me, "O Daniel, man greatly beloved, understand the words that I speak to you, and stand upright, for I have now been sent to you." While he was speaking this word to me, I stood trembling.**

Then he said to me, "Do not fear, Daniel, for from the first day that you set your heart to understand, and to humble yourself before your God, your words were heard; and I have come because of your words. But the prince of the kingdom of Persia withstood me twenty-one days; and behold, Michael, one of the chief princes, came to help me, for I had been left alone there with the kings of Persia. (Daniel 10:11-13).

In Daniel's case there was a twenty-one day delay before he received the answer. A spiritual warfare was taking place in the unseen realm of which he was not aware. However, an angel was sent to Daniel with the answer to his earnest seeking of the Lord while he was engaged in prayer and fasting. But this angel was prevented from completing his mission until he received help from another powerful angelic being known as Michael. What lessons can we learn from this today? First, God will *always hear* the earnest sincere prayer—otherwise Jesus' exhortation to His followers to pray would not make sense. Second, we must not think God hasn't heard our prayers simply because we do not see an immediate answer. In Luke 18 Jesus taught a parable to emphasize the necessity of consistent persevering prayer encouraging us that we **"always ought to pray and not lose heart"** (Luke 18:1). In other words, as we pray we must keep believing, or as one pastor says it, we should "Stay in faith."

Jesus also exhorted us to **"Watch and pray, lest you enter into temptation"** (Matthew 26:41). Of course, there is someone who would like us to give up and discontinue our prayers of faith—Satan, the enemy of God's people. So obeying the command of Jesus to **"watch and pray"** by keeping alert and not allowing the influence of the world, the flesh and the devil to distract us, we can overcome the temptation to not press forward in persistent prayer. If we feel we are being attacked by Satan and are tempted to give up seeking the Lord, it may well be because Satan knows the answer is on the way if we will keep on in faith. It would be a shame and a loss to give up when the answer is right on our doorstep! No, we pray because we *know* God hears and answers our prayers.

I cannot think of anything that would be more thrilling, than to know that through this gift of prayer I have personal contact with the Creator of the universe. Of course, it would obviously be more thrilling to be in His presence for eternity in the new heavens and earth, but while I am still in the body on this earth it is awesome to know I already have such wonderful access to my Heavenly Father through Jesus my Lord. An important Scripture we must include in this chapter is 1 Timothy 2:1-4:

Therefore I exhort first of all that supplications, prayers, intercessions, *and* **giving of thanks be made for all men, for kings and all who are in authority** [or prominent place of service], **that**

we may lead a quiet and peaceable life in all godliness and reverence** [or dignity]. **For this *is* good and acceptable in the sight of God our Savior, who desires all men to be saved and to come to the knowledge of the truth."**

God will hear and answer sincere prayers for all the areas of life mentioned by Paul in this list written to Timothy. Prayers are to be offered for **"all men"** but especially for those in legal authority over us. I believe one of the great lacks in many Christians' prayer lives concerns the very things mentioned in this verse. When I became an American citizen many years ago I had to learn about the Constitution and the different branches of government. I learned about the Rule of Law making it clear that even those in positions of authority and leadership had themselves to abide by the established laws of the land. Since we have these laws and the elected leaders who thus have authority over us, it makes sense that we should take the matter seriously to pray for them **"that we may lead a quiet and peaceable life."**

Do we want America to change for the good so that we can live this kind of life? The question is: Do we really believe our prayers can make a difference? If we really understood the vicious battle that is raging for the future of our country we will pray and fast as we may never have done before. If this battle is lost, the principles of righteousness and justice upon which this nation was founded will produce an America that Christians will definitely not like. The vision of our founders will have dissipated and disappeared in an increasing vortex of corruption deserving of judgment like that brought upon Sodom and Gomorrah.

The verse above reminds us that God **"desires all men to be saved."** Since this is His revealed will, we should be praying for the salvation of our leaders and all those around us. We should be praying for those who influence through the media and for teachers who teach our young. We should be praying specifically for God to give unsaved men and women windows of opportunity for them to sense the drawing of the Holy Spirit. The only way for this nation to change for the better is for individuals to be brought to salvation one by one.

If we are using the faith God provides for us through His Word we should expect amazing answers to our prayers. Do we have enough faith for another spiritual renewal in America? How could such an awakening possibly happen in a society that seems to have lost its way spiritually and morally? It could happen because our God actually hears and answers the earnest prayers of His people—if only we will pray.

We should be praying on a regular basis for God the Holy Spirit to bring true conviction of sin wherever needed. This is absolutely vital if true repentance is to be experienced by those who are presently lost spiritually. But repentance is also surely needed among those of us who claim to be God's people, for it is through true believers God will work to minister the convicting work of the Holy Spirit to those around us. Yes, if we really want God to hear from heaven we must come to Him in His way and on His terms.

The prophet Elijah knew the God who hears and answers prayer. Because of the ungodly King Ahab and his wife Jezebel who had killed some of the Lord's prophets (1 Kings 18:4), God led Elijah to prophesy there would be a drought. The nation of Israel as a whole had forsaken worship of the true God, and were worshiping Baal, the false pagan god of the Canaanites. They believed Baal controlled the weather for the benefit of their crops. But God fulfilled the prophecy of Elijah and there was no rain on the land for three-and-a-half years, thus exposing Baal as a false god. James summarizes this event by writing:

"The effective fervent prayer of a righteous man avails much. Elijah was a man with a nature like ours, and he prayed earnestly that it would not rain; and it did not rain on the land for three years and six months. And he prayed again, and the heaven gave rain, and the earth produced its fruit" (James 5:16-18).

How earnestly did Elijah pray? We get insight into this by noticing how he prayed for rain after the three-and-a-half years of drought. Here again is the account mentioned earlier:

And Elijah went up to the top of Carmel; then he bowed down on the ground, and put his face between his knees, and said to his servant, "Go up now, look toward the sea." So he went up and looked, and said, "There is nothing." And seven times he [Elijah] said, "Go again." Then it came to pass the seventh *time* **that he said, "There is a cloud, as small as a man's hand, rising out of the sea!" So he said, "Go up, say to Ahab, 'Prepare** *your chariot,* **and go down before the rain stops you.'"**

Now it happened in the meantime that the sky became black with clouds and wind, and there was a heavy rain (1 Kings 18:42-45).

We see two main things in this incident with Elijah. First, the need for persistence in prayer. Second, there may be a shorter or longer period of time before the answer is experienced in reality. Because we live in twenty-first-century culture we generally expect our desires and wants to be satisfied quickly. However, when it comes to spiritual things such as answers to prayer we must remember that God is never too late and His timing will always be sufficient to meet the need. Therefore, when we are confident of praying according to His will we should never allow the enemy to trick us into giving up.

We need the exhortation to pray earnestly and passionately for another spiritual awakening in America because it is desperately needed. We must mean business with God if we expect an ingathering of souls into the kingdom of God. This can happen even while outwardly things in our nation would appear to be getting worse. This is exactly what the Bible predicts through the Apostle Paul when he wrote,

"But know this, that in the last days perilous times will come: For men will be lovers of themselves, lovers of money, boasters, proud, blasphemers, disobedient to parents, unthankful, unholy, unloving, unforgiving, slanderers, without self-control, brutal, despisers of good, traitors, headstrong, haughty, lovers of pleasure rather than lovers of God . . . But evil men and impostors will grow worse and worse, deceiving and being deceived" (2 Timothy 3:1-4,13).

The point is, we should never look at the outward situation of evil and ungodliness and throw up our hands in despair. Who would have thought before they occurred that the great awakenings of the past would have happened? No, it took spiritual men and women with vision and persistent faith in prayer for the tides to turn and waves of Holy Spirit conviction to bring revival and salvation to so many.

Can God do it again? Absolutely! But will God find enough of His people in America with enough determination to seek Him with the prayer and faith He is looking for? At this time of our great need as a nation, it is the only way to see another great spiritual move of God to change the hearts of thousands with true salvation? This is why I believe God has led me to write this book. Will you join me in passionate prayer for God's hand to bless this nation once more? Perhaps you would like to stop reading right now, and if possible, spend some time in earnest prayer for God's mercy to be granted to our nation.

CHAPTER 8

AND WILL FORGIVE THEIR SIN

Sin! Is there sin in the Church? Have we become soft on sin in order not to offend anyone? Are preachers, ministers and Bible teachers more concerned about the amount of money in the collection plate than about the spiritual condition of those they are supposed to serve? Do we even hear the word *sin* biblically expounded from most pulpits today? Are preachers too afraid of losing tithe-paying members to preach on the doctrine of sin?

Sin is not what some may consider to be just little human mistakes that God will overlook. Sin is a serious matter—extremely serious. It has everything to do with eternal consequences. It will divide the human race and decides the destinies of individuals to forever reside in either heaven or hell. Ever since the first sin of disobedience in the Garden of Eden humans have suffered from the effects of its plague.

Sin afflicts every soul on the face of this earth—even including those infants who have inherited the sinful nature but are not yet guilty until they reach the age of accountability. As people who claim to be followers of Jesus Christ, sin is our enemy. We would wish that we did not sin, but we do. The Apostle John wrote, **"If we say we have no sin, we deceive ourselves, and the truth is not in us"** (1 John 1:8). He recognized that the temptations we all face from the world, the flesh, and the devil are very real and dangerous. He makes this plain as he gives instructions regarding these threefold antagonists to remind us of the spiritual pitfalls inherent in them:

"Do not love the world or the things in the world. If anyone loves the world, the love of the Father is not in him. For all that *is* in the world—the lust of the flesh, the lust of the eyes, and the pride of life—is not of the Father but is of the world. And the world is passing away, and the lust of it; but he who does the will of God abides forever" (1 John 2:15-17).

In contrast to these threefold agents of temptation that influence us away from a life pleasing to God, John reminds us that it is only the person who **"does the will of God"** who will be prepared for eternity. Somehow we must learn to **"not love the world or the things in the world."** In other words, our love cannot be divided if we want to be the persons God wants us to be and enjoy to the fullest our relationship with Him. Our enemy knows our weak points intimately. Therefore, he will do his best with the aid of his demonic agents to cause us to do exactly the opposite of the exhortation John gives in the scripture above.

The *world* in general is not godly, but evil. Let me be blunt and honest. If an apparently innocent involvement in activities like sports, hobbies, or the sciences, completely engulfs our interest and time to the extent that we live only for these things, they become sin to us. I have often thought of some in fields of science who devote their whole lives to the study of nature, animals, or perhaps just one type of animal such as a beetle. What a tragedy and what eternal regrets will be theirs when they stand before God, and realize to their chagrin they have missed the whole purpose of their earthly existence—for the sake of studying the intricacies of beetles! Actually, the amazing design found even in beetles should have led such a person to the realization that there must be a Creator. From the perspective of eternity this is why the Bible reminds us of the importance of seriously considering how we spend our time. I will repeat a few verses included in chapter four which relate to the importance of time taken for prayer, and now for their connection to sin:

"See then that you walk circumspectly [carefully]**, not as fools but as wise, redeeming the time, because the days are evil** (Ephesians 5:15,16).

"Walk in wisdom toward those *who are* **outside, redeeming the time"** (Colossians 4:5).

We certainly don't want to be **"fools"** as Paul wrote above. But we need to be wise, and one of the most important ways to be wise is to understand what sin is and the need for forgiveness. It becomes a dangerously deceptive problem when we sin but do not recognize the significance of what we are doing, or how living with sin in our lives will affect us negatively both now and in the future.

This is where the importance of self examination becomes a vital exercise we need to apply to ourselves with complete transparency. Our enemy, Satan, would love for us to become involved in something we have been deceived to look upon as harmless and acceptable before God, but is actually sin. For example, we may be deceived to think a short two or three minute prayer to God is sufficient for each day. It will be a huge shock to many a professed Christian to suddenly discover that such a lack of prayer and communion with God can be seen as sin. The great devotional expositor Andrew Murray writes powerfully about this:

> "If conscience is to do its work, and the contrite heart is to feel its misery, it is necessary that each individual should mention his sin by name. The confession must be severely personal. In a meeting of ministers there is probably no single

sin which each one of us ought to acknowledge with deeper shame—'Guilty, verily guilty'—than the sin of prayerlessness. What is it, then, that makes prayerlessness such a great sin? At first it is looked upon merely as a weakness. There is so much talk about lack of time and all sorts of distractions that the deep guilt of the situation is not recognized. Let it be our honest desire that, for the future, the sin of prayerlessness may be to us truly sinful" (Andrew Murray. *The Prayer Life.* Moody Press, Chicago, 1982 15).

Some may find it hard to believe that prayerlessness is a sin as Murray describes it, and think of it as too strong a concept to accept. But he continues by making four more vigorous statements regarding prayerlessness:

1. "WHAT A REPROACH IT IS TO GOD.—There is the holy and most glorious God who invites us to come to Him, to hold converse with Him, to ask from Him such things as we need, and to experience what a blessing there is in fellowship with Him. He has created us in His own image, and has redeemed us by His own Son, so that in converse with Him we might find our highest glory and salvation."
2. "IT IS THE CAUSE OF A DEFICIENT SPIRITUAL LIFE.—It is a proof that, for the most part, our life is still under the power of *the flesh* . . . ."
3. "THE DREADFUL LOSS WHICH THE CHURCH SUFFERS AS A RESULT OF PRAYERLESSNESS OF THE MINISTER.—It is the business of the minister to train believers up to a life of prayer; but how can a leader do this if he himself understands little the art of conversing with God and of receiving from the

Holy Spirit, every day, out of heaven, abundant grace for himself and for his work?"
4. "THE IMPOSSIBILITY OF PREACHING THE GOSPEL TO ALL MEN—as we are commanded by Christ to do—so long as this sin is not overcome and cast out" (Andrew Murray. *The Prayer Life.* Moody Press, 1982 15-19. *Emphasis by the author*).

Powerful words! Do the Scriptures support what he has written? Did Jesus actually command us to pray? Consider these scriptures:

"Watch and pray, lest you enter into temptation. The spirit indeed *is* willing, but the flesh *is* weak" (Matthew 26:41).

"But I say to you, love your enemies, bless those who curse you, do good to those who hate you, and pray for those who spitefully use you and persecute you" (Matthew 5:44).

"And when you pray, you shall not be like the hypocrites. For they love to pray standing in the synagogues and on the corners of the streets, that they may be seen by men. Assuredly, I say to you, they have their reward" (Matthew 6:5).

"But you, when you pray, go into your room, and when you have shut your door, pray to your Father who *is* in the secret *place;* and your Father who sees in secret will reward you openly" (Matthew 6:6).

"And when you pray, do not use vain repetitions as the heathen *do.* For they think that they will be heard for their many words" (Matthew 6:7).

"In this manner, therefore, pray: Our Father in heaven, Hallowed be Your name" (Matthew 6:9).

Then He said to them, "The harvest truly *is* great, but the laborers *are* few; therefore pray the Lord of the harvest to send out laborers into His harvest" (Luke 10:2).

"Watch therefore, and pray always that you may be counted worthy to escape all these things that will come to pass, and to stand before the Son of Man" (Luke 21:36).

When He came to the place, He said to them, "Pray that you may not enter into temptation" (Luke 22:40).

"Rejoicing in hope, patient in tribulation, continuing steadfastly in prayer" (Romans 12:12).

"What is *the conclusion* then? I will pray with the spirit, and I will also pray with the understanding. I will sing with the spirit, and I will also sing with the understanding" (1 Corinthians 14:15).

"And take the helmet of salvation, and the sword of the Spirit, which is the word of God; praying always with all prayer and supplication in the Spirit, being watchful to this end with all perseverance and supplication for all the saints—and for me, that utterance may be given to me, that I may open my mouth boldly to make known the mystery of the gospel" (Ephesians 6:17-19).

"Be anxious for nothing, but in everything by prayer and supplication, with thanksgiving, let your requests be made known to God" (Philippians 4:6).

"Continue earnestly in prayer, being vigilant in it with thanksgiving" (Colossians 4:2).

"**. . . pray without ceasing**" (1 Thessalonians 5:17).

"**Therefore I exhort first of all that supplications, prayers, inter-cessions,** *and* **giving of thanks be made for all men**" (1 Timothy 2:1).

"**I desire therefore that the men pray everywhere, lifting up holy hands, without wrath and doubting**" (1 Timothy 2:8).

"**Confess** *your* **trespasses to one another, and pray for one another, that you may be healed. The effective, fervent prayer of a righteous man avails much**" (James 5:16).

"**But the end of all things is at hand; therefore be serious and watchful in your prayers**" (1 Peter 4:7).

"**But you, beloved, building yourselves up on your most holy faith, praying in the Holy Spirit**" (Jude 1:20).

"**And the smoke of the incense, with the prayers of the saints, ascended before God from the angel's hand**" (Revelation 8:4).

Can we now see quite clearly how the scriptures tell us unequivocally that prayer is to be a vital and continuous practice for the Christian? What better good thing can we do during our short stay on this earth than to be faithful in prayer to the One who created us? James 4:17 says, **"Therefore, to him who knows to do good and does not do it, to him it is sin."**

So all we have said so far supports the teaching that it would be correct and scriptural to call prayerlessness a sin as does Andrew Murray. This is most likely to be an alarming realization for many Christians. What is the remedy? It is to humbly repent of this lack in our lives and set about to adjust our lifestyles to incorporate real meaningful communion with the Lord on a regular basis. When it is revealed to us that we need to repent we need to remember God's wonderful grace to forgive. The Apostle John wrote**, "If we confess our sins, He is faithful and just to forgive us *our* sins and to cleanse us from all unrighteousness"** (1 John 1:9). When we realize the error of our ways the thing to do is not to despair, but repent, know that we are forgiven, make necessary corrections and know that we can continue from this point with a commitment to a new start. God corrects us because He loves us.

It will not be easy at first if a five-minute prayer and Bible reading has been our regular or irregular habit. But as we continue with sincere motivation to put God first in our lives we will find our desire for a closer relationship with the Lord growing stronger and stronger. In fact, from my own experience I can verify that as you continue to be faithful in spending time with the Lord you will look forward to these times with great anticipation and desire. You will not want to miss your secret rendezvous with the Lord, and will sense a loss if circumstances cause you to miss this sacred time of communion with your Creator. And most exciting and rewarding, you will see God answer your prayers as you believe with the faith He has given you.

America needs forgiveness, and God has already provided for such. If we have become so desensitized to our sinful failures as a nation and do not discern the need for forgiveness, we are in a sorry state of spiritual blindness indeed. Just as God's Word says, **"But evil men and impostors will grow worse and worse, deceiving and being deceived"** (2 Timothy 3:13). So although America is still a great place to live compared to many other countries, we are deeply concerned to have seen evil increase exponentially over recent years. How are people who are living sinful lifestyles—dare I even say professing Christians—going to come to the place where they realize their need to repent and ask God for forgiveness? There is only one scriptural way, and this is through the ministry of the Holy Spirit bringing guilt to the surface which will cause individuals to realize their sinful state before God.

In my opinion it is a terrible deception when professed Christians, including pastors and those in spiritual leadership, can nonchalantly declare that God understands their sinful weaknesses and overlooks them. The most obvious example would be those living in open immorality such as adulterers and homosexuals, which, unbelievably and totally without scriptural support, are finding acceptance in some churches today. We should be interceding in prayer for the full and complete ministry of the Holy Spirit to be manifestly evident throughout the body of Christ across our country. Jesus points to the answer of how sin should be dealt with when He talked about the ministry of the Holy Spirit:

"And when He has come, He will convict the world of sin, and of righteousness, and of judgment: of sin, because they do not believe in Me; of righteousness, because I go to My Father and you see Me no more; of judgment, because the ruler of this world is judged" (John 16:8-11).

Professing Christians in America desperately need the powerful convicting work of the Holy Spirit to prick their consciences as individually appropriate. This can lead to a renewal and deepening of a relationship with the Lord as sin is dealt with through the application of Christ's sacrifice on the cross. With such a renewal the Christians' testimony before the world can become more powerful and effective as the Holy Spirit moves through them with His convicting ministry. This is sorely needed because the spirit of the world in unbelievers is to deny the existence of sin. Even some professed Christians can be deceived into thinking they can participate in sin without suffering the consequences. Some Bible teachers today have taken the truth of the grace of God beyond what the Word teaches. It is still true both for the saved and unsaved that each will reap what they have sown (See Galatians 6:7).

Sadly, there are countless stories of Christians in leadership and ministries of all kinds who have fallen into disgrace after having been deceived by the subtleties of sinful temptation. They have not followed the example of Jesus by resisting the enemy with the Word of God (See Matthew 4:1-11). We have a perfectly holy and righteous God, and only those who have the covering of the righteousness of Christ can approach Him in reverential confidence. But those who are deceived by sin are walking on ice so thin that if they continue in sin the ice will crack under them, and they will fall into a lost eternity unless God is able to draw them to Himself by His grace. James 5:19,20 which is written to Jewish believers says,

"Brethren, if anyone among you wanders from the truth, and someone turns him back, let him know that he who turns a sinner from the error of his way will save a soul from death and cover a multitude of sins."

Yes, we desperately need the convicting power of the Holy Spirit to cause us to come to our senses and bow in humility and repentance before a Holy God. Over a hundred years ago the powerful evangelist D. L. Moody wrote the following:

"If you go back to the Scripture records, you will find that the men who lived nearest to God, and had most power with Him, were those who confessed their sins and failures . . . I firmly believe that the Church of God will have to confess her own sins, before there can be any great work of grace. There must be a deeper work among God's believing people. I sometimes think it is about time to give up preaching to the ungodly, and preach to those who profess to be Christians.

If we had a higher standard of life in the Church of God, there would be thousands more flocking into the Kingdom. So it was in the past; when God's believing children turned away from their sins and their idols, the fear of God fell upon the people round about. Take up the history of Israel, and you will find that when they put away their strange gods, God visited the nation, and there came a mighty work of grace" (D. L. Moody, *Prevailing Prayer,* Moody Press, Chicago, circa 1889 25,26).

Even in Moody's time he saw great spiritual lack in the church as a whole, and wondered if he should not concentrate on ministering to professed Christians rather than the ungodly. Meanwhile, the Lord was using him in ministry to the unsaved with thousands responding to the gospel he preached. Yes, if there is sin in the Church, and there surely is, it needs to be confessed and repented of in all sincerity and humbleness. In fact, from Jesus' teaching and the example of the early first century Church, it would be very appropriate to seek God with prayer accompanied with fasting. On January 23, 1996, a pastor from Wichita, Kansas, Joe Wright, prayed a prayer that got everybody's attention at the new session of the Kansas state senate:

Heavenly Father, we come before you today to ask your forgiveness and to seek your guidance. We know your Word says, "Woe to those who call evil good," but that is exactly what we have done.

We have lost our spiritual equilibrium and inverted our values.

We confess that we have ridiculed the absolute truth of your Word and called it moral pluralism.

We have worshipped other gods and called it multiculturalism.

We have endorsed perversion and called it alternative lifestyle.

We have exploited the poor and called it the lottery.

We have rewarded laziness and called it welfare.

We have killed our unborn and called it choice.

We have shot abortionists and called it justifiable.

We have neglected to discipline our children and called it building self-esteem.

We have abused power and called it political savvy.

We have coveted our neighbor's possessions and called it ambition.

We have polluted the air with profanity and pornography and called it freedom of expression.

We have ridiculed the time-honored values of our forefathers and called it enlightenment.

    Search us, Oh God, and know our hearts today; try us and see if there be some wicked way in us; cleanse us from every sin and set us free. Guide and bless these men and women who have been sent here by the people of Kansas, and who have been ordained by you, to govern this great state. Grant them the wisdom to rule and may their decisions direct us to the center of your will. I ask it in the name of your Son, the living Savior, Jesus Christ. Amen (*Journal of the Senate,* Kansas Legislature 1995-1996, Topeka, Kansas, January 23, 1996, 2).

This prayer was a shock to those who were there and heard it, and then later to everyone when it was made public. Pastor Wright hung out America's sins for all to hear. The truth hurts, but being honest should help us to see the need more clearly and drive us to our knees.

Now here is the good news: God forgives. This is an amazing statement. Why should God even consider forgiving rebellious, disobedient sinful creatures like ourselves? Because God is love! In His infinite wisdom God created us as humans in His image for a higher purpose than the rest of His creation. I sometimes remind visitors on a tour of our museum, that God did not create monkeys for the purpose of having fellowship with them. No, it is for the purpose of having amazing intimate fellowship with us that He created us in His image, and we are the only living beings on earth who have such an awesome privilege and possibility. This distinction is clearly seen in Genesis 1:26,27 which reads:

Then God said, "Let Us make man in Our image, according to Our likeness; let them have dominion over the fish of the sea, over the birds of the air, and over the cattle, over all the earth and over every creeping thing that creeps on the earth." So God created man in His *own* image; in the image of God He created him; male and female He created them.

Yet, we know our ancestor Adam failed God in the Garden of Eden which caused separation from Him and brought death into the world. Romans 5:12 reminds us,

"Therefore, just as through one man sin entered the world, and death through sin, and thus death spread to all men, because all sinned."

But because of God's love He provided a plan and a way for His creation to be forgiven from the very beginning. This was only to be through the shedding of innocent blood which represents life, and such would provide the possibility of forgiveness and reconciliation with Him in fellowship. Adam and Eve lost that fellowship and relationship with God, and found themselves forced outside the garden never able to return.

However, just before they were made to leave the garden God showed them very vividly His ordained way for ultimate acceptance into His presence. Genesis 3:21 tells us, **"Also for Adam and his wife the Lord God made tunics of skin, and clothed them."** This tells us the innocent life's blood of a creature (perhaps a lamb) had to be shed, and as God clothed Adam and Eve with these skins it pictured God's incredible plan of salvation for the future. God has provided for today's believers to be clothed with the righteousness of God through the once and for all sacrifice of Jesus on the cross. No longer is there any need to sacrifice the blood of animals. The joyous news today is that *we can be forgiven*. All made possible because the Father loves us so much He was willing to give His Son Jesus to be the ultimate blood sacrifice for us.

Does this incredible blessing happen automatically in our lives? No. We must approach God in the way our key scripture for this book directs us:

"If My people who are called by My name will humble themselves, and pray and seek My face, and turn from their wicked ways, then I will

hear from heaven, and will forgive their sin and heal their land" (2 Chronicles 7:14).

There are great and grievous sins existing in American culture today. Without question we are guilty before God, and need to come before Him in humility to seek His forgiveness for our sins, and to seek for a spirit of repentance to be found in us. If we let the Holy Spirit lead us in such a seeking of God He will be found of us, and He will forgive us. The price has been paid! Then we can pray with the faith of Elijah for healing, renewal and revival in this highly favored land of ours.

CHAPTER 9

AND HEAL THEIR LAND

The best solution for sickness is healing! Have you noticed that America is plagued with serious sicknesses? Even in a Bible-belt *nice* area of the Midwest like Springfield, Missouri, the daily news is a series of never-ending tragedies. There are constant reports of murders, shootings, drug busts, robberies, domestic violence, sex crimes of all kinds, violent protests, along with pervasive general discontent and anger in the lives of many people.

You might be tempted to think that I live in a terrible place. But this is not unique to the Springfield area, because the same scenario is happening in cities all over America. What has brought about such change in this country that such evil and sinful behavior has become so prevalent? It is obvious that local authorities do not have answers to the enormity of the problem, and our brave police are stretched beyond their limits to try and keep law and order.

What is the solution? Have things become too complex in our modern society that hope for a solution seems impossible and unrealistic? Yes, the America I found when I emigrated here from England in 1963 is hugely different today, and not for the better. There has been a continual, subtle, ungodly force exerted on the culture that has changed the very atmosphere of our country. Our Founding Fathers would be dismayed and shocked at the degenerative influences filling our airwaves through public media, the anti-God teachings taking place in our educational institutions, and yes, especially the effect on many who are addicted to so-called smart phones, which Satan is using in clever ways to influence and lead people into innovative ways of sinning. It is not *smart* to allow modern technology to steal our minds and time away from the important things of life that have to do with eternal realities—such as building up our spiritual lives through prayer and the Word of God. Yet, in spite of all the obvious negatives, God has given us this seemingly unrealistic promise in His Word that a sinful nation such as ours can be healed if the conditions He has given us are fulfilled.

If God's people are willing to fulfill these conditions He has given us we can certainly hope for improvement, but it will probably come in ways we do not expect. Who, except a few with prophetic insight, would have expected Donald Trump to become America's president in 2017? If God is giving America a season of reprieve as some godly people are suggesting, then we the Church—God's people—desperately need to get on board during this unique and opportune moment of time we find ourselves part of today. The Bible says, **"Behold, now *is* the accepted time; behold, now *is* the day of salvation."** (2 Corinthians 6:2).

This is surely the time to engage in earnest prevailing prayer for God's guidance in the Church and for individual Christians. It is time to seek the fullness of His presence in our lives, and in His strength we can then obey our Lord's commission to reach the lost with the gospel. In other words, as God's people we are to be revived with the zeal and passion of the Holy Spirit to affect the communities we live in. We must acknowledge and understand the reality of the warfare we are engaged in—which is a fierce battle for the survival of an America whose foundation was based on the Christian biblical values of righteousness, integrity and justice.

The enemy of God, Satan, is exerting every effort through the means he has available to bring America down. He hates America in a similar way to his hatred of

Israel, which is because the Son of God came to this earth as a descendent of Abraham and defeated Satan by His victorious sacrifice and resurrection over death. Satan hates the godly influence, although certainly not always predominant, that has been in America since its inception. His work and desire is to influence ungodly people to serve him without them realizing what they are doing and how they are being deceived. Jesus said, **"Walk while you have the light, lest darkness overtake you; he who walks in darkness does not know where he is going"** (John 12:35). People are walking in the darkness of deceptive influence that hinders them from being able to see the truth about the purpose of their existence.

This cunning deception that works so well for Satan has been his mode of operation from the beginning of creation. Eve fell for it, and then Adam willingly went along with disobedience to God which resulted in death, suffering and destruction becoming the norm in our world. The Apostle Paul wrote,

"Therefore, just as through one man sin entered the world, and death through sin, and thus death spread to all men, because all sinned . . . For we know the whole creation groans and labors with birth pangs together until now" (Romans 5:12; 8:22).

Adam and Eve needed healing, and as we said earlier, the only way for healing to begin was by the sacrifice of innocent blood. But sin in the form of domestic violence soon brought tragedy to that first family when Cain killed his brother Abel. And the presence of evil continues to this day unabated unless there will be a gracious move of God's Spirit to bring conviction, repentance and salvation through faith in Christ.

There is a basic scientific principle accepted by scientists which is known as the law of cause and effect. Wherever we see an effect, there will be a cause with one exception—God. We believe God is eternal and uncaused. Therefore, when we observe America today with all its problems, which are effects, we know there has to be a cause. Some would immediately think I should say many causes rather than cause, but biblically speaking we can narrow the ills of America to one cause, sin. Not only America, but the whole world as the Apostle John writes, **"We know that we are of God, and the whole world lies *under the sway of* the wicked one"** (1 John 5:19).

If sin is the problem, and I believe the Scriptures confirm this, there obviously needs to be a consciousness of it in the hearts and minds of God's people. Without this there will not be a sense of the need for confession and repentance. Before we can hope to see whole communities affected by gracious revivals with souls coming into the kingdom and experiencing salvation, professed Christians must come before God to find out what their standing is with Him. If this is done honestly and transparently before the Lord, I see hope for spiritual healing to take place across this country.

Can you imagine how wonderful it would be to see our police having less and less problems with those who get into trouble because of their sinful tendencies? This actually happened during the Hebrides revival described in chapter four above. As many were saved the very atmosphere on the islands changed. Jails were emptied as crimes decreased and liquor stores actually went out of business because their clientele disappeared.

Such things could only begin to happen if we, God's people, will do what He has challenged us to do—to humble ourselves, pray, seek His face, turn from our wicked ways, be forgiven and see God begin to work in our communities for good. But remember, it is going to be a battle. The enemy is not going to like any move toward revival and he not going to stand by and do nothing to prevent it. He will do his best to dissuade Christians from seeking God fervently in prayer, and will especially try to discourage prayer accompanied with fasting. But if we really mean business with God we should be willing to use every means available to get ourselves positioned before God so we can be useful servants by bearing fruit for Him. This is the purpose of prayer with fasting, to get ourselves right before God by getting rid of baggage we don't need in order to be pure vessels for His service.

America desperately needs the healing touch of an awakening which can literally change the atmosphere of communities across this land. Only the reality of God's supernatural presence invading thousands upon thousands of individual lives will bring such a dramatic change. We have allowed the devil far too much freedom to wreak havoc across this beautiful land, and now we have the challenge from God to be part of an amazing spiritual revolution which can set the Church on fire with Holy-Spirit zeal and usher thousands, even millions into the kingdom of God. It has happened in the past, and God can certainly do it again. But it depends on us. Are we willing, and do we have the desire to pay the price for such change? We know the truth, and we know what to do, but are we willing to be like Esther of old and recognize that God has allowed us to be here **"for *such* a time as this"**? (Esther 4:14).

Will God find enough righteous in our land to avert judgment and destruction? We are crippling ourselves as a nation by being at war with ourselves. I was watching on TV the path of the lunar eclipse which took place on August 21, 2017. Apparently the path of this eclipse was unique and rare because it crossed the entire width of the United States from the northwest to the southeast. As I was watching the thought came to me that just as the eclipse appears to divide America, so we are literally divided as a nation. We are divided as liberals and conservatives politically, but the most significant division is that which divides the righteous from the unrighteous, the saved from the spiritually lost.

As I wrote above, if the unrighteous outnumber the righteous in our nation it should wake us up as Christians to the desperate urgent need for a new spiritual awakening. I heard a youth pastor speak a message in which he told a group of enthusiastic young people what the secret was in order for them to change the world. He referenced the Old Testament story of Daniel and noted that he did not compromise his stand for God and truth. Part of the account reads:

But Daniel purposed in his heart that he would not defile himself with the portion of the king's delicacies, nor with the wine which he drank; therefore he requested of the chief of the eunuchs that he might not defile himself (Daniel 1:8).

Daniel made a commitment from the heart. He wanted to stay pure before God and was willing to do so at all costs. He did not want to defile himself, but I'm afraid that today many professed Christians are defiling themselves with the influence of the secular ungodly world around them. If we don't spend that crucial quiet time alone with God on a regular basis we will be weak and tend to let the world, the flesh, and the devil influence us rather than us influencing the people around us. This is how our land can be healed, by community after community being affected by Christians who live the abundant life in Christ of victorious, Spirit-led, holy living. I have to believe that God wants to heal our land and see His people enjoying the privilege and experience of a wonderful intimate relationship with Him. If we will do what God says by seeking Him with all of our hearts, I believe we can see these changes begin to take place. The Apostle John wrote, **"And this is the victory that has overcome the world—our faith"** (1 John 5:4).

We must believe. We must have daily faith in the presence of Christ living within us by the Holy Spirit— **"Christ in you, the hope of glory"** (Colossians 1:27). If we pray and believe, we will see God answer our prayers in amazing ways. Yes, we can see the miracle of change and healing take place in America. Next we will read how we can and should be part of God's plan.

CHAPTER 10
BEING A PART OF GOD'S PLAN

What an awesome privilege it is for us as Christians to be part of God's plan for reaching people with His truth during our earthly lives. Every Christian should realize and believe that God has a specific personal plan for his or her life. We are all a vital part of His team. We did not choose where we were born or who our parents were, but in God's providence we can be exactly who God wants us to be where He has positioned us in life. I can say with absolute confidence, that God wants all of us to be fruitful in our lives for our own blessing, for the betterment of those around us, and for the influence of the gospel throughout our country.

America is in such a crucial and disastrous situation as I write. This is mainly because we Christians have allowed Satan to gain many footholds into our society which has caused evil to triumph on many fronts. A state senator working in Jefferson City, Missouri, has stated on social media that she wished someone would assassinate president Trump! Surely an example of freedom of speech at its worst! Police are being shot and killed on a regular basis. America's racial and ethnic problems are boiling and bursting at the seams with rioting, physical violence and hatred.

What is the answer to such evil influence and lawlessness? What are Christians to be doing individually in the face of such demonic influence? The beginning of the answer is not complicated: We must get on board with God's plan for reaching those walking in spiritual darkness with the love of Jesus Christ through the power of the Holy Spirit. If we will pray and witness to unbelievers as the Scriptures tell us we should, we can begin to see a change in communities across our land. America seems to be at an eleventh-hour critical turning point. There are the God-given possibilities of either proceeding with passionate prevailing prayer to see wholesome change and victories for the kingdom of God, or losing this opportunity and watching our country crash into the depths of ungodliness, rejection and judgment by God.

To put all this another way, the biblical way, if we are to see good things begin to happen we must obey what the Lord has told His people to do according to His revealed plan of action when He explained,

"But you shall receive power when the Holy Spirit has come upon you; and you shall be witnesses to Me in Jerusalem, and in all Judea and Samaria, and to the end of the earth" (Acts 1:8).

The plan for His Church has not changed, and it means that all of us as Christians, with no exceptions, are to be His Spirit-led witnesses. We are all called just as the early disciples were to give **"witness to the resurrection of the Lord Jesus"** (Acts 4:33). This is what our witness is supposed to be and to accomplish if we are truly part of His team and part of His plan. But we should notice carefully an exceedingly important prerequisite the Lord spoke of in order for us to be successful witnesses. This is something all Christians desperately need if the Church is truly the salt and light in our society the Lord has called us to be for Him. Question: Is there something missing in the lives of many good Christians that hinders the effectiveness of their witness? Yes, the scripture above identifies the problem clearly.

The only biblical way for Christians to be effective through their witness is to have the indwelling spiritual power of the Holy Spirit. Some of us may need to go beyond denominational teachings that ignore or overlook this truth that we need the power that comes only from the fullness of the Holy Spirit to fulfill God's calling in our lives. It is not the purpose of this writing to go into the scriptural support for the fact that a Christian can experience the indwelling of the Holy Spirit but still lack the anointing of power. But this is what is so desperately needed in each of our lives individually. We should all examine ourselves (as does this writer), to see if we live in the **"power"** Jesus talked about which should be present in the real experiences of our daily lives. Dr. Wilbur M. Smith, deeply concerned about the spiritual lack of the Church's power for witness wrote the following in 1945:

> Our Lord promised the Church that on the day when it should be born, it would have an anointing of power from God. I have heard a great many sermons, and read a great many pages on this promise of power through the Holy Spirit, but generally I feel that the meaning here has been missed. Men seem to pray for power in preaching, that they themselves might be dynamic, or unusually influential from the pulpit, capable of moving audiences, perhaps fluent in speech, etc., etc. Now, all this is all right, but the reason why the early church had to have *power,* divine power, was because of the many enormous powers which it had to overcome, powers which were holding the souls and minds and hearts of men in their fearful grip. There was to begin with, the power of sensuality, the power of the flesh; there was the power of idolatry, with all of its show and appeal, its temples and priesthood, things that could be touched and seen and heard; there was the power of paganism, mastering the Mediterranean world for centuries; there was the power of the

increasing tendency on the part of Roman rulers to be looked upon as God, and the determination of the Roman government to enforce such demonic deification; there was the power of false philosophy, and all the philosophic schemes which had been born and had flourished in the early Greek and later Roman world; there was the power of darkness, the sheer weight of despair and hopelessness; and finally, there was the power of demons, and all the Satanic agencies which could be mustered by the arch-enemy of God and His gospel. If these early Christians had not had power, divine power, power greater than all the antagonistic powers in the world put together, the gospel would have been doomed from the first day of its declaration.

It is this power that we need now, in the face of an increasing antagonism toward Christian faith, an antagonism that is as powerful now as in the days of the early church—with this profound difference, that the ancient pagan world was weary of the failure and acknowledged futility and foolishness of its attempts to find God and to be delivered from sin, and was ripe for the proclamation of a divine message, whereas today, after 1900 years of the gospel, there is a mysteriously accelerated drifting away from the gospel, the truth of which can never be disproved, back into myths similar to those held in the ancient world at the time of our Lord's advent, or, into worse, an utter indifference to everything concerning God, even to the denial of the soul which can know God" (Wilbur M. Smith, *Therefore Stand,* W. A. Wilde Co., Natick, Mass. 1945 507-508).

As mentioned above, this was written in 1945! Dr. Smith died in 1976 and had served as Professor of Apologetics at Fuller Theological Seminary in Pasadena, California. He could have written this today if he was living, for our situation in America has not become any better. If fact, as we all know, it has become unbelievably much worse. Yes, we desperately need to have the dynamic power, the real power of the Holy Spirit if we are to see the Church gain victories over the world, the flesh, and the devil in our country today.

A PERSONAL TESTIMONY

When I think of my earlier life before I became a Christian, I remember how I was blest at the age of ten to find myself in contact with believers through a Sunday afternoon Bible class for boys. A few years later when about the age of thirteen, a school friend invited me to a local Sunday school and church where I heard the gospel and surrendered my life to Christ. However, at that young age I had some real fears and had no idea how to overcome them—especially speaking in public. From my earliest memories up to and after I became a believer in Christ, I was always extremely shy and reserved in social settings—a real introvert. Even after joining the British Royal Air Force at age nineteen I would literally be terrified with my heart pounding at the thought of having to say anything publicly. Obviously, I wanted to overcome this intimidation and fear of expressing myself, but I had no idea how to go about it.

However, it was during my time spent stationed on the Mediterranean island of Cyprus that I had a special visitation from God, which turned out to be a life-changing experience for me. After studying the Bible with the help of a friend, I came to the point of believing that God promises all His followers a wonderful gift Jesus calls being baptized in the Holy Spirit (I found out later the word *immersed* is a better translation than the word *baptized*). Even though I was a born-again Christian and had been attending church regularly all my teenage years since becoming a believer, this knowledge about the Holy Spirit was something completely new to me.

As I began to pray for more of the Holy Spirit in my life I discovered that the ultimate answer to my prayer was to arrive at a place spiritually where I would let the Holy Spirit have *more of me*. Look again at the sentence you have just read and notice that the emphasis is on the Holy Spirit having *more of me* rather than me having the Holy Spirit's presence in my life without evidence of spiritual power. In other words, the Holy Spirit needs to be free to flow through my being without hindrance in order to fulfill His purpose in me.

This is beautifully pictured in the Psalms when David wrote, **"You anoint my head with oil; my cup runs over"** (Psalm 23:5). There was a need for me to learn to come before the Lord with real earnestness and desire with the right motives as I continued seeking Him. I had to be transparently willing to let the Holy Spirit deal with me and expose any lack in my life I wasn't aware of, and then I would need to surrender unconditionally to Him in those areas.

As I continued with these times of seeking the Lord through prayer and meditation in His Word, I began to realize I was coming into a closer and more intimate relationship with Him than I had ever known before. This continued for about five or six weeks, during which time I was thrilled with the blessings of experiencing more and more joy, peace, and an increasing sense of His real presence in my life. I would go to the little chapel on the base every chance I got, often into the night hours when no one else was around. Then one day as I was praying with a friend the Holy Spirit suddenly immersed me in

His presence. I literally felt an incredible warmth that seemed to begin in the depths of my being and spread over my whole body. This was just like Jesus had predicted to His disciples about the coming of the Holy Spirit when He said,

"If anyone thirsts, let him come to Me and drink. He who believes in Me, as the Scripture has said, out of his heart (belly, KJV) will flow rivers of living water" (John 7:37,38).

Tears of joy were cascading from my eyes as I realized the Lord was granting my requests. How true the scripture is that says, **"Then you will call upon Me and go and pray to Me, and I will listen to you. And you will seek Me and find *Me*, when you search for Me with all your heart"** (Jeremiah 29:12,13).

After this experience I was certainly enjoying a spiritual high. My seeking and searching for the blessing of the Lord had reaped the result of a more personal intimate relationship with the Lord than I had ever experienced before. But did this blessing from the Lord help solve my intimidation problem in social settings? Absolutely! It wasn't long before I found myself giving Bible studies and speaking before small groups. Not only was I not afraid to speak publicly, but I actually wanted to share the Word of God at every opportunity. In fact, one of my friends on the base also had a similar experience with the Holy Spirit, and during those days we saw a number of young men respond to the gospel and become believers. We observed in a small way what the Holy Spirit could do through believers who were surrendered in their hearts to be part of God's plan for the spreading of the good news of the gospel. There was definitely a spirit of revival amongst us during those days.

Question: Are we willing to fit into God's plan for us even if the very thought of doing so causes some apprehension in our thinking? I remember a statement I heard many years ago that is not in the Bible but certainly agrees with biblical truth: God's calling is God's enabling. In other words, God would not expect us to accomplish something He does not give us the strength and power to fulfill. But He does expect from us that which is according to His plan and purpose for us individually. Jesus talked about salt and light as illustrations to help us understand His plans for us:

"You are the salt of the earth; but if the salt loses its flavor, how shall it be seasoned? It is then good for nothing but to be thrown out and trampled underfoot by men. "You are the light of the world. A city that is set on a hill cannot be hidden. Nor do they light a lamp and put it under a basket, but on a lampstand, and it gives light to all *who are* in the house. Let your light so shine before men, that they may see your good works and glorify your Father in heaven" (Matthew 5:13-16).

Jesus reminds us that salt can lose its flavor. Can Christians also lose their spiritual flavor, and, alarming thought, **"be good for nothing"**? Jesus warns that a light can be kept hidden and therefore would not serve its purpose. Are there professed Christians who are not being godly influences to those around them. Are there those in the Church who are not making an effort with the Lord's help, to penetrate the darkness in this present world with the light and presence of the Lord from within them? As a writer I have to look at my own life when I write words such as these, and realize my need to come before the Lord with transparency and humility and let Him show me how I can become a more fruitful member of His team. I have no excuse to offer if I am not what I should be as one who professes to be a disciple of Christ.

God has supplied all the means and provision if I will avail myself of such, and as I do I will become the person He wants me to be as part of His team on earth. When our Lord called His original disciples He issued a simple but powerful invitation with these words:

And Jesus, walking by the Sea of Galilee, saw two brothers, Simon called Peter, and Andrew his brother, casting a net into the sea; for they were fishermen. Then He said to them, "Follow Me, and I will make you fishers of men." They immediately left *their* **nets and followed Him. Going on from there, He saw two other brothers, James** *the son* **of Zebedee, and John his brother, in the boat with Zebedee their father, mending their nets. He called them, and immediately they left the boat and their father, and followed Him** (Matthew 4:18-22).

Peter, Andrew, James and John were willing to leave their nets and boats. Some would say this represents a call to fulltime service and does not mean that all Christians should leave their jobs, houses and possessions to serve the Lord. This is true, but are not all of us called into fulltime service even though we work at the same time to earn a living? Absolutely, and the Lord will show each of us how this can be worked out in our individual lives. However, the **"nets"** and **"boats"** the early disciples left behind could symbolize things in our lives as Christians which hinder our effectiveness and witness for the Lord. For example, how much money do we spend on unnecessary luxuries that have absolutely no value for enhancing our influence for the Lord? When we are blest with financial provision and blessing do we ask the Lord to help us be good stewards of the resources He has given us? Do we tend to be a little too careful in our conversation with our neighbors lest they think we are too spiritual? Are we too timid to speak about spiritual things with our unsaved relatives in order to prevent them and us from feeling uncomfortable? Do we actually show more love and concern for our pet animals than we do for the unsaved? Or, in general, what does the way we live reveal about how much we love God and our neighbors? Jesus said,

"You shall love the Lord your God with all your heart, with all your soul, and with all your mind. This is the first and great commandment. And the second is like it; you shall love your neighbor as yourself. On these two commandments hang all the law and the prophets" (Matthew 22:37-40).

The only people God wants on His team are those who are ardently earnest and passionate about their relationship with Him. Notice the four times the word *all* is used by Jesus in the above scripture. God loves His creation, and even offers His love to those who are opposed to Him. As Christians we are supposed to be vessels through which the love of God flows through as we witness to the unsaved. The Bible says,

"The Lord is not slack concerning *His* promise, as some count slackness, but is longsuffering toward us, not willing that any should perish but that all should come to repentance" (2 Peter 3:9).

Notice again the word *all* in this verse, which tells us that as God's messengers we have been given the privilege and task of reaching those God's wants to save. The only way for this to be accomplished to any degree is by fitting into His plan for us to be His willing servants and carriers of the Gospel.

If we are filled and immersed in His love we will gladly be willing participants in the carrying out of His plan. However, living our lives selfishly with no involvement or interest in being a part of His plan will put us in the rejection zone—a dangerous place to be! Instead, let us continue with faith for God to use us for His glory in any way He chooses.

CHAPTER 11
BOUGHT TO SERVE

We have all probably heard someone say with a negative attitude: I just don't have a life of my own anymore. Is this something we would expect a dedicated Christian to say? No, because what we should be doing if we are sincere disciples of Jesus Christ, is to recognize the glorious privilege it is to be His servants and give of our time, energy, and strength to His service. If we don't, we will have regrets in the future for a life lived that was meaningless and of no lasting eternal value. The Apostle Paul wrote,

"Or do you not know that your body is the temple of the Holy Spirit *who is* in you, whom you have from God, and you are not your own? For you were bought at a price; therefore glorify God in your body and in your spirit, which are God's" (1 Corinthians 6:19,20).

If we think we should be the ones to have total control of our own lives we have not discovered the joy of surrender to a wonderful loving God who knows what is best for us. No, we should not think of ourselves as being our own independent selves. We are here to **"glorify God."** We belong to the One who was willing to shed His blood on a tortuous cross that we might be forgiven, cleansed, and lifted up from the bondage and control of sin. We will never fully comprehend what it meant to God the Father to love His wayward creation so much He was willing to give part of Himself, Jesus, God the Son, to suffer an ignominious, humiliating, and horrific crucifixion in order to defeat the curse of death. He did it for you and me. The Apostle Peter makes it plain,

"You were not redeemed with corruptible things, *like* silver or gold, from your aimless conduct *received* by tradition from your fathers, but with the precious blood of Christ, as of a lamb without blemish and without spot" (1 Peter 1:18,19).

And the Apostle Paul states,

"Christ has redeemed us from the curse of the law, having become a curse for us (for it is written, 'Cursed *is* everyone who hangs on a tree'), that the blessing of Abraham might come upon the Gentiles in Christ Jesus, that we might receive the promise of the Spirit through faith" (Galatians 3:13,14).

The whole purpose of what God has done for us through the cross is to restore the beautiful fellowship that was broken in the Garden of Eden. He has lovingly opened the way for this relationship with Him to be realized, but we are the ones who must decide whether to take advantage of such a gracious offer or live to regret it forever. Remember, the choice is either revival or rejection!

God has responded to us of His own volition, but now we need to respond to Him. Is revival for America something God will bring upon us as a nation arbitrarily without our involvement? Of course not! God does not have us on strings as puppets. He wants our willing participation, and if we will fulfill the conditions as clearly described in His Word, He will be faithful to bless us according to His promises.

For those who have been influenced to take the doctrine of the sovereignty of God beyond what Scripture teaches, this is not revival by *works*. It is revival by willing cooperation with God according to His promises, and by doing our part through seeking Him earnestly as

He has exhorted us to do in His Word. When we consider the extreme sacrificial price Jesus paid for our salvation, we should passionately desire to see corresponding fruit reaped as a result and benefit for His great sacrifice.

Jesus has made it clear that as His followers we should never expect to sit around without being involved in a ministry of some kind. Even Adam and Eve were required to take care of the land with its thorns and thistles after they were expelled from the Garden of Eden. It is expected of us to bear fruit for the kingdom of God. In John's Gospel chapter fifteen Jesus gives us an illustration to show how our relationship with Him should produce beneficial and eternal results:

"I am the true vine, and My Father is the vinedresser. Every branch in Me that does not bear fruit He takes away; and every *branch* that bears fruit He prunes, that it may bear more fruit" (John 15:1,2).

Let me remind us that in this scripture Jesus is not teaching by a parable or by allegory, but more by analogy—using similarity for comparison. Taking the scripture at face value He is using the grape vine and the branches to emphasize a real and literal relationship between Himself and those individuals who profess to believe in Him. Again, some of us may have to go beyond our particular denominational background teaching to avoid eisegesis—making scriptures like this to mean what we would prefer them to mean. Because when Jesus says **"Every branch in Me"** unfortunately some will attempt to interpret this as not referring to a true believer. But this is hard to do because in verse five Jesus says to his believing disciples, **"I am the vine, you *are* the branches. He who abides in Me . . ."** Note the personal pronoun, **"He."** Therefore using standard exegesis—understanding the words grammatically, the words of Jesus **"in Me"** refer to a real intimate and personal relationship. Simply, this means that to be a true disciple and able to bear the right kind of spiritual fruit, we must be *in Him* by intimate spiritual relationship. This also means that true spiritual activity leading to effective witness for the Lord must involve God's presence and power flowing *through us* and *from us* to those in our circle of influence. We cannot bring conviction of sin and reach into the heart of people to encourage repentance by our own persuasive methods, it must be by the ministry of the Holy Spirit. Jesus also said, **"He who abides in Me, and I in him, bears much fruit; for without Me you can do nothing"** (John 15:5).

If it is true, and it is, that we can do nothing by ourselves without the dynamic presence of the Holy Spirit, what exactly is left for us to do that we can do? The problem is that many of us feel the urge to *do something* for God, which is commendable, but we must come to the point of realization that God knows what is best for us to do and when to do it. Jesus put it this way when His disciples asked Him how they could be involved in the work of God,

"Then they said to Him, "What shall we do, that we may work the works of God?" Jesus answered and said to them, "This is the work of God, that you believe in Him whom He sent" (John 6:28,29).

This is the secret of honoring our Lord in thankfulness for His great sacrifice for us, and understanding how He wants us to live for Him as His servants; it is to *believe*. Well, we may say we believe in Him, but the question we need to ask is: Do we really believe for Him to minister from *within us* and *through us*? The Apostle Paul prayed for the Christians at

Ephesus **"that Christ may dwell in your hearts through faith"** (Ephesians 3:17). It is by **"faith"** that the presence of Christ dwells within us in reality.

God is looking for those who truly believe. Our Christian *works* done through the enthusiasm of busy activity and carnal motives without the leading of the Holy Spirit, will produce a spiritual deadness that hinders our witness rather than enhancing it. Our *service of works* carried out as ministry for the Lord must be Holy-Spirit inspired, led, and empowered. This is the *only way* to produce fruit that is beneficial and of lasting eternal value. For example, do we think those Jews who heard the Apostle Peter speaking on the Day of Pentecost were thinking mainly about Peter as a person? No, they were convicted by the Holy Spirit not because of their exposure to Peter personally as a prophetic spokesman, but because *through* Peter the powerful anointing of the Holy Spirit was reaching into their hearts.

The scriptures from John fifteen mentioned above should be considered with all seriousness by taking the meaning of Jesus' words at face value. They are not difficult to understand providing we don't confuse ourselves with theological opinions from certain commentators, who struggle to explain how to keep the meaning of these scriptures within the bounds of their particular stream of predetermined belief. Unfortunately, this is so easy for all of us to do, so I am attempting to encourage us to consider the whole counsel of God by asking the Holy Spirit to do exactly what Jesus said He would do,

"However, when He, the Spirit of truth, has come, He will guide you into all truth; for He will not speak on His own *authority,* but whatever He hears He will speak; and He will tell you things to come" (John 16:13).

This is an amazing and awesome truth. We are not left to our own unreliable and fallible mental resources, but have available to us God the Holy Spirit to lead us **"into all truth."**

The subject of this chapter reminds us that we have been purchased by the precious blood of Jesus. As His possessions, that is, if we willingly surrender to His working in and through our lives, He has a particular plan and purpose for all of us individually. He will guide us and lead us into the great privilege of serving Him in the work of the kingdom of God. If we claim to be His servants but bear absolutely no fruit of any kind for the kingdom of God, we could be in a precarious and spiritually dangerous situation. We cannot play games with God! With solemn and alarming words Jesus said,

"Every branch in Me that does not bear fruit He takes away; and every *branch* that bears fruit He prunes, that it may bear more fruit" (John 15:2).

Jesus paid an incomprehensible price for our redemption, and it is only right and to be expected that those receiving the benefits of such an amazing sacrifice, should respond by willingly giving of their lives to bear fruit for Him. Let's imagine for a moment that if a branch could talk it might say: If you don't mind, I would rather live my life as a branch the way I choose without having to feel restricted by what you (the vine) want me to do. We can immediately see by utilizing the same illustration of the vine and branches as Jesus did the absolute foolishness of such an attitude. We can also see again that God's main purpose for His creation is without variation always about relationship. We can never be a *branch* pleasing to Him unless we accept the closeness and intimacy with Him that He wants us to have. Is God really serious about this? Absolutely!

According to the straightforward understanding of the words of Jesus above, branches (professed believers) who do not bear any fruit **"He takes away."** Obviously a branch (Christian) cannot be taken away from the vine unless it (he or she) has been attached by believing. John 15:6 expresses the same thought using the illustration of a branch becoming withered.

"If anyone does not abide in Me, he is cast out as a branch and is withered; and they gather them and throw *them* into the fire, and they are burned."

Obviously, if we choose (and it is a free-will choice) not to **"abide"** (Greek: *remain*) in relationship with Him there could be disastrous eternal implications (more on this important truth is for another writing in the future as the Lord allows). I would not like to become a **"withered"** branch with loss of the beautiful personal relationship always available for me because of His love and sacrifice for me.

How should we show our appreciation to the Lord for His wonderful grace and dealings in our lives? How can we make sure we *remain in Him*, bear fruit, and not be taken away from Him or become a withered branch? We must take advantage of His offer to have that personal intimate relationship with Him. He says to those who professed to believe in Him at the Laodicean Church,

"Behold, I stand at the door and knock. If anyone hears My voice and opens the door, I will come in to him and dine with him, and he with Me" (Revelation 3:20).

God has already made the first move toward us, and now it remains to see if we will move toward Him. He gives us this awesome privilege. How do we do this?

By spending quality time in prayer and by meditating, studying, and absorbing His living Word into our beings. If we do this with a sincere heart, I believe we will experience Spirit-led fruit-bearing service for our Lord. This will bring glory to His name and to His great sacrifice for us on the cross. Have you prayed and read the Word of God today?

CHAPTER 12

HIS LEADING NOT MINE

You and I have a choice to make. We can either determine to follow God's direction for our lives, or we can ignore His leading and go our own way in life and reap the consequences. It should be obvious to us which is the better choice, but because of our tendency to want to order our own lives, the choice is most often not an easy one. Because of America's present situation of unrest, turmoil, and spiritual cultural warfare, it is vital that true believers in Jesus Christ and the gospel should determine to follow the way God would lead and guide.

When it comes to something as dramatic as having faith for a sweeping national revival, there are many mountains of opposition that appear, with daunting pathways to ascend and overcome before we can begin to approach the summit and see the reality of revival. David Ravenhill, the son of well-known revivalist Leonard Ravenhill wrote the following:

> Our choice is simple: We either repent and cry out to God for mercy or face the wrath of God as He promised so long ago. I was pleasantly surprised to hear while visiting Singapore recently that there were many churches there who prayed earnestly for our presidential election last year. The tragedy, though, was to have to tell them I knew very few congregations in America who set time aside to pray for our own election.
>
> Prior to my father's death in '94, he would say, "If America doesn't concentrate in prayer, they will pray in concentration camps." President Trump was elected to govern in the natural arena; the

church was birthed to govern in the spiritual realm. Our power and authority is far greater than any Congress, Senate, Supreme Court or president. If we fail to take our place, America will miss her day of visitation, like Jerusalem of old. It's time to rise up and take our rightful place before the throne of God and implore God for a mighty move of His Spirit. Revival or revolution? The church will decide.

(www.charisma.com/opinion/66967 accessed 8-25-17)

I'm sure that some would feel Ravenhill went too far when he suggested American Christians could one day find themselves interred in concentration camps! But doesn't the Bible tell us of Christians who ended up in prison because they faithfully followed the Lord's leading in their lives and ministry? Absolutely, and it would be nothing new. Those early Christians and others since the founding of the Church had spiritual backbone enough to put the Lord and His plan for their lives first and foremost, regardless of the persecution and suffering they endured.

Some may question if these experiences of Christians down through the years were just the result of natural cause and effect—that their zealous witnessing, and not God's specific leading caused the reaction of those around them. But the Bible tells the truth when referring to suffering saints in previous times. They suffered because of their *faith in God's purpose, plan and leading in their lives.* In the Book of Hebrews we read of a variety of things that happened to many of God's faithful saints. It says,

"Who through faith subdued kingdoms, worked righteousness, obtained promises, stopped the mouths of lions, quenched the violence of fire,

escaped the edge of the sword, out of weakness were made strong, became valiant in battle, turned to flight the armies of the aliens. Women received their dead raised to life again. Others were tortured, not accepting deliverance, that they might obtain a better resurrection. Still others had trial of mockings and scourgings, yes, and of chains and imprisonments.

They were stoned, they were sawn in two, were tempted, were slain with the sword. They wandered about in sheepskins and goatskins, being destitute, afflicted, tormented—of whom the world was not worthy." (Hebrews 11:33-38).

We must realize that in any kind of warfare there are usually casualties on both sides as seen in this scripture. Are we afraid of martyrdom? Could things actually come to this in America? When we read an account like this from Scripture it should really make us ashamed that we have had it so easy and blest in this country, and at the same time so many of us have tended to rest on our laurels by not being the light and salt we are called to be, and should have been. We are the ones responsible for giving the enemy leeway to infiltrate our culture with sin and ungodliness.

Somewhere along the way we have missed God's leading. We are the ones who have let both God and ourselves down, and are reaping the results in America today in ways that cause us distress of heart and mind because of the increase of evil and ungodliness. However, when things look bad there is always the possibility of a turnaround. For the ancient people of Israel one of the times of distress they experienced was during the time Saul was king. The Philistines, ever a thorn in the side of God's people, were challenging Israel through Goliath, one of their giant heroes. Of all the army of Saul, no one felt the leading of God or had the courage to face up to Goliath. And no wonder, for he was physically powerful and over nine feet tall. It took a youthful David, who instead of being intimidated by the size of Goliath, was more impressed with the power and greatness of his God. Louie Giglio writes about this:

> "Can you imagine what that must have been like? Chances are, we've been in the midst of a righteous army that lifts a war cry but remains immobilized by the taunts of the Enemy. That's what some churches look like today. We gather each Sunday and lift up powerful anthems of worship to our God. That's our war cry. We position ourselves for battle. We claim the victory. We might even shout down the Devil. But that's as far as we ever get. When the Sunday service is over, the same giant steps up and defies the power of God to keep us and save us and transform us" (Louie Giglio, *Goliath Must Fall,* HarperCollins Christian Publishing, Inc. 2017 63,64).

Ungodly America is a huge giant to deal with. If Christians will rise up like David with God's divine power behind us, we could see the spiritual giant's head of ungodliness restrained or even decapitated. Satan hates anything that is good about America—especially dedicated Christians who live holy lives, pray, know their Bible, and witness for the truth. We should be willing to ask ourselves a powerful but uncomfortable question: Is the Church more concerned about being rejected by the world than being rejected by God? We must mean business with God! If there is to be victory for the proclaiming of the gospel with multitudes coming into the kingdom of God, we must be earnest and passionate in our faith or it will not happen.

Another powerful thought to consider is whether

the Church in general considers itself to be in the driver's seat or under God's authority. Who is the Head of the Church? Jesus Christ, but is He allowed to be who He is? When there is bickering and disagreement over theology, church procedures, worship modes, and a host of other issues, it must be that the leading and direction of the Holy Spirit is missing or not being followed. Both individually and as the body of Christ, we should all be totally submissive and humble before God by recognizing His rightful authority over us in all of our ways. If we do this in all honesty and sincerity of heart I believe we will see the power of God defeat the enemy on many fronts—both individually, and corporately as the Church.

Yes, we need the attitude of David to have faith that God is with us and is more powerful than all the host of hell combined. This is how we should look at the *Goliath* of the sad state of America today. Is there an answer? Of course! With God there is always an answer if we will approach Him in submission to His Word. A very special scripture to me personally, and one I have quoted to myself almost constantly for many years is Psalm 25:4,5 which reads:

"Show me Your ways, O Lord; Teach me Your paths. Lead me in Your truth and teach me, for You *are* the God of my salvation; On You I wait all the day."

The first thing I think about from the words of this prayer, is that we should not pray it, cannot really pray it, unless we have truly put ourselves in a teachable position before the Lord. He will not show us His ways for us if we come with any other attitude. We must be totally open and willing to be taught. He is the Teacher by His Holy Spirit, and we can ask and expect Him to show us the path He wishes for us to travel in our daily walk both individually and corporately. We have all been taught many things by different people, but we must be discerning about what we hear and with an open heart pray, **"Lead me in Your truth and teach me."** It is *His truth* we need, not man's often fallible interpretations. In my book *Walking With God* I wrote the following about our need to follow the leading of the Lord in our lives:

> God is calling us to walk in His will, but have we come to the place of personal committal and total surrender to that will? There should be a practical application of His will to our daily lives. Or, in other words, the course of our daily lives should be directed by the Lord, and not by ourselves. It is one thing to mentally grasp a knowledge and understanding of His will, His calling, and His legitimate demands upon our lives, but another thing entirely to completely submit to Him in these crucial matters.
>
> Finding that desirable, **"...good and acceptable and perfect will of God"** (Romans 12:2), involves personal choice. Oh, how momentous, serious, and of inestimable importance to us both now and for all eternity are the choices we make today! We can set our own course which will ultimately result in grievous and sorrowful regrets, or we can choose the crucified life in Christ which will lead to blessing and glory beyond our ability to conceive or imagine. (Rod Butterworth, *Walking With God*. Word Alive Press, Winnipeg, 2003 229-233).

Following is a list of scriptures concerning God's ways and promises to lead us through the experiences of our lives. I suggest reading these verses out loud slowly and prayerfully. As you read them it will inspire faith to face any challenges you may encounter during your Christian walk:

"Lead me, O LORD, in Your righteousness because of my enemies; make Your way straight before my face" (Psalm 5:8).

"I will bless the LORD who has given me counsel; my heart also instructs me in the night seasons. I have set the LORD always before me; because He is at my right hand I shall not be moved" (Psalm 16:7,8).

"You will show me the path of life; in Your presence is fullness of joy; at Your right hand are pleasures forevermore" (Psalm 16:11).

"May He grant you according to your heart's desire, and fulfill all your purpose" (Psalm 20:4).

"The LORD is my shepherd; I shall not want. He makes me to lie down in green pastures; He leads me beside the still waters. He restores my soul; He leads me in the paths of righteousness for His name's sake" (Psalm 23:1-3).

"Show me Your ways, O LORD; Teach me Your paths. Lead me in Your truth and teach me, for You are the God of my salvation; On You I wait all the day" (Psalm 25:4,5).

"Good and upright is the LORD; Therefore He teaches sinners in the way. The humble He guides in justice, and the humble He teaches His way" (Psalm 25:8,9).

"Teach me Your way, O LORD, and lead me in a smooth path, because of my enemies" (Psalm 27:11).

"For You are my rock and my fortress; therefore, for Your name's sake, lead me and guide me." (Psalm 31:3).

"My times are in Your hand; deliver me from the

hand of my enemies, and from those who persecute me" (Psalm 31:15).

"I will instruct you and teach you in the way you should go; I will guide you with My eye. Do not be like the horse or like the mule, which have no understanding, which must be harnessed with bit and bridle, else they will not come near you" (Psalm 32:8,9).

"Delight yourself also in the LORD, and He shall give you the desires of your heart. Commit your way to the LORD, trust also in Him, and He shall bring it to pass. He shall bring forth your righteousness as the light, and your justice as the noonday. Rest in the LORD, and wait patiently for Him" (Psalm 37:4-7).

"The steps of a good man are ordered by the LORD, and He delights in his way. Though he fall, he shall not be utterly cast down; for the LORD upholds him with His hand" (Psalm 37:23,24).

"Wait on the LORD, and keep His way, and He shall exalt you to inherit the land" (Psalm 37:34).

"I waited patiently for the LORD; and He inclined to me, and heard my cry. He also brought me up out of a horrible pit, out of the miry clay, and set my feet upon a rock, and established my steps" (Psalm 40:1,2).

"Oh, send out Your light and Your truth! Let them lead me; let them bring me to Your holy hill and to Your tabernacle" (Psalm 43:3).

"For this is God, our God forever and ever; He will be our guide even to death" (Psalm 48:14).

"God is our refuge and strength, a very present

help in trouble. Therefore we will not fear, even though the earth be removed, and though the mountains be carried into the midst of the sea" (Psalm 46:1,2).

"Hear my cry, O God; attend to my prayer. From the end of the earth I will cry to You, when my heart is overwhelmed; lead me to the rock that is higher than I" (Psalm 61:1,2).

"My soul, wait silently for God alone, for my expectation is from Him. He only is my rock and my salvation; He is my defense; I shall not be moved"(Psalm 62:5,6).

"Nevertheless I am continually with You; You hold me by my right hand. You will guide me with Your counsel, and afterward receive me to glory" (Psalm 73:23,24).

"Give ear, O LORD, to my prayer; and attend to the voice of my supplications. In the day of my trouble I will call upon You, for You will answer me" (Psalm 86:6,7).

"Teach me Your way, O LORD; I will walk in Your truth" (Psalm 86:11).

"And let the beauty of the LORD our God be upon us, and establish the work of our hands for us" (Psalm 90:17).

"Blessed is the man whom You instruct, O LORD, and teach out of Your law" (Psalm 94:12).

"My eyes shall be on the faithful of the land, that they may dwell with me; he who walks in a perfect way, he shall serve me" (Psalm 101:6).

"I called on the LORD in distress; the LORD answered me and set me in a broad place. The

LORD is on my side; I will not fear. What can man do to me?" (Psalm 118:5,6).

"Blessed are the undefiled in the way, who walk in the law of the LORD! Blessed are those who keep His testimonies, who seek Him with the whole heart! They also do no iniquity; they walk in His ways. You have commanded us to keep Your precepts diligently. Oh, that my ways were directed to keep your statutes"! (Psalm 119:1-5).

"Make me walk in the path of Your commandments, for I delight in it" (Psalm 119:35).

"I thought about my ways, and turned my feet to Your testimonies" (Psalm 119:59).

"Teach me good judgment and knowledge, for I believe Your commandments"

(Psalm 119:66).

"Your word is a lamp to my feet and a light to my path" (Psalm 119:105).

"I am Your servant; give me understanding, that I may know Your testimonies" (Psalm 119:125).

"The LORD shall preserve your going out and your coming in from this time forth, and even forevermore" (Psalm 121:8).

"The LORD will perfect that which concerns me; Your mercy, O LORD, endures forever; do not forsake the works of Your hands" (Psalm 138:8).

"If I take the wings of the morning, and dwell in the uttermost parts of the sea, even there Your hand shall lead me, and Your right hand shall hold me" (Psalm 139:9,10).

"Search me, O God, and know my heart; try me,

and know my anxieties; and see if there is any wicked way in me, and lead me in the way everlasting" (Psalm 139:23,24).

"Cause me to hear Your lovingkindness in the morning, for in You do I trust; cause me to know the way in which I should walk, for I lift up my soul to You. Deliver me, O LORD, from my enemies; in You I take shelter. Teach me to do Your will, for You are my God; Your Spirit is good. Lead me in the land of uprightness" (Psalm 143:8-10).

"He stores up sound wisdom for the upright; He is a shield to those who walk uprightly; He guards the paths of justice, and preserves the way of His saints. Then you will understand righteousness and justice, equity and every good path" (Proverbs 2:7-9).

"Trust in the LORD with all your heart, and lean not on your own understanding; in all your ways acknowledge Him, and He shall direct your paths" (Proverbs 3:5,6).

"Do not be afraid of sudden terror, nor of trouble from the wicked when it comes; for the LORD will be your confidence, and will keep your foot from being caught" (Proverbs 3:25,26).

"I have taught you in the way of wisdom; I have led you in right paths. When you walk, your steps will not be hindered, and when you run, you will not stumble" (Proverbs 4:11,12).

"But the path of the just is like the shining sun, that shines ever brighter unto the perfect day" (Proverbs 4:18).

"Ponder the path of your feet, and let all your ways be established. Do not turn to the right or the left; remove your foot from evil" (Proverbs 4:26,27).

"For the ways of man are before the eyes of the LORD, and He ponders all his paths" (Proverbs 5:21).

"The integrity of the upright will guide them" (Proverbs 11:3).

"The righteousness of the blameless will direct his way aright" (Proverbs 11:5).

"Where there is no counsel, the people fall; but in the multitude of counselors there is safety" (Proverbs 11:14).

"Commit your works to the LORD, and your thoughts will be established" (Proverbs 16:3).

"A man's heart plans his way, but the LORD directs his steps" (Proverbs 16:9).

"A man's steps are of the LORD; how then can a man understand his own way?" (Proverbs 20:24).

"Many people shall come and say, come, and let us go up to the mountain of the LORD, to the house of the God of Jacob; He will teach us His ways, and we shall walk in His paths" (Isaiah 2:3).

"This also comes from the LORD of hosts, who is wonderful in counsel and excellent in guidance" (Isaiah 28:29).

"Your ears shall hear a word behind you, saying, 'This is the way, walk in it,' whenever you turn to the right hand or whenever you turn to the left" (Isaiah 30:21).

"Thus says the LORD your Redeemer, the Holy One of Israel: 'I am the LORD your God, who teaches you to profit, who leads you by the way you should go' " (Isaiah 48:17).

"The LORD will guide you continually, and satisfy your soul in drought, and strengthen your bones; you shall be like a watered garden, and like a spring of water, whose waters do not fail" (Isaiah 58:11).

"They shall come with weeping, and with supplications I will lead them. I will cause them to walk by the rivers of waters, in a straight way in which they shall not stumble" (Jeremiah 31:9).

"Therefore I will look to the LORD; I will wait for the God of my salvation; my God will hear me" (Micah 7:7).

"But while he thought about these things, behold, an angel of the Lord appeared to him in a dream, saying, 'Joseph, son of David, do not be afraid to take to you Mary your wife, for that which is conceived in her is of the Holy Spirit' " (Matthew 1:20).

"Therefore do not worry about tomorrow, for tomorrow will worry about its own things. Sufficient for the day is its own trouble" (Matthew 6:34).

"Ask, and it will be given to you; seek, and you will find; knock, and it will be opened to you. For everyone who asks receives, and he who seeks finds, and to him who knocks it will be opened" (Matthew 7:7,8).

"He went a little farther and fell on His face, and prayed, saying, 'O My Father, if it is possible, let this cup pass from Me; nevertheless, not as I will, but as You will.'" (Matthew 26:39).

"And behold, there was a man in Jerusalem whose name was Simeon, and this man was just and devout, waiting for the Consolation of Israel, and the Holy Spirit was upon him. And it had been revealed to him by the Holy Spirit that he would not see death before he had seen the Lord's Christ. So he came by the Spirit into the temple..." (Luke 2:25-27).

"Then Jesus, being filled with the Holy Spirit, returned from the Jordan and was led by the Spirit into the wilderness." (Luke 4:1).

"Jesus said to them, 'My food is to do the will of Him who sent Me, and to finish His work'" (John 4:34).

"I can of Myself do nothing. As I hear, I judge; and My judgment is righteous, because I do not seek My own will but the will of the Father who sent Me" (John 5:30).

"If anyone wills to do His will, he shall know concerning the doctrine, whether it is from God or whether I speak on My own authority" (John 7:17).

"However, when He, the Spirit of truth, has come, He will guide you into all truth; for He will not speak on His own authority, but whatever He hears He will speak; and He will tell you things to come" (John 16:13).

"Then the Spirit said to Philip, 'Go near and overtake this chariot'" (Acts 8:29).

"After they had come to Mysia, they tried to go into Bithynia, but the Spirit did not permit them...And a vision appeared to Paul in the night...Now after he had seen the vision, immediately we sought to go to Macedonia, concluding that the Lord had called us to preach the gospel to them" (Acts 16:7,9,10).

"Then he [Ananias] said [to Paul], 'The God of our fathers has chosen you that you should know His will, and see the Just One, and hear the voice of His mouth' " (Acts 22:14).

"For as many as are led by the Spirit of God, these are sons of God" (Romans 8:14).

"I have been crucified with Christ; it is no longer I who live, but Christ lives in me; and the life which I now live in the flesh I live by faith in the Son of God, who loved me and gave Himself for me" (Galatians 2:20).

"But if you are led by the Spirit, you are not under the law" (Galatians 5:18).

"For the Lamb who is in the midst of the throne will shepherd them and lead them to living fountains of waters. And God will wipe away every tear from their eyes" (Revelation 7:17).

What wonderful inspiration comes from meditating on scriptures such as these. Question: Do we really believe these truths with all of our hearts? It is only as these truths are applied to our lives in reality without doubting that we will experience the blessing of them. May each of us seek and allow the Lord to lead us according to His plan for our lives. If we do, we will surely have cause for much rejoicing in the future. Next we will learn more of God's desire to manifest His power through our lives.

CHAPTER 13

HIS POWER, NOT MINE

"The chief danger that confronts the coming century will be RELIGION WITHOUT THE HOLY SPIRIT, Christianity without Christ, forgiveness without repentance, salvation without regeneration, politics without God, and heaven without hell." William Booth, 1829-1912, founder of the Salvation Army.
(www.goodreads.com/author/quotes/151267.William Booth, accessed 9-25-17, emphasis mine)

William Booth's warning written over one hundred years ago is even more relevant today than in his times. If we desire a revival with genuine salvations affecting millions of people across America, the first thing we should know is that in and of ourselves we cannot generate such a move of God. After the tragedy of 9-11-2001 in New York City there was a sudden increase in church attendance, but it only lasted a matter of months. Many have ridiculed the suggestion that what happened at that time was some kind of judgment of God on our nation. Can we prove that it wasn't? No! However, when we recognize how America has from the highest levels of government approved lifestyles and passed laws that the Bible clearly indicates are sinful and detestable to God, I would have to say that the shoe of judgment fits.

We know it is a historical fact that God brought judgment on Israel in the past because they turned their back on Him and worshiped false gods, so why should we think America is immune to such judgment? However, because of the prophecies of Jesus concerning the last days before His coming, it is to be expected that calamities of many kinds will afflict earth and its peoples—such as earthquakes, hurricanes, volcanoes, and nations rising against one another in war. Whether from other countries or from within America we see evil people who are doing evil things. This is the sad story of humanity, and of course, it began in the Garden of Eden with disobedience to God. We continue to reap the sad consequences of sin which the world still experiences to this day. The Apostle Paul confirmed this present scenario with these words,

"For the earnest expectation of the creation eagerly waits for the revealing of the sons of God. For the creation was subjected to futility, not willingly, but because of Him who subjected *it* **in hope; because the creation itself also will be delivered from the bondage of corruption into the glorious liberty of the children of God. For we know that the whole creation groans and labors with birth pangs together until now"** (Romans 8:19-22).

When Paul writes about the **"bondage of corruption"** he is referring to the imperfect world resulting from the original sin in the Garden of Eden which affects all of nature and humankind. Yes, many are *groaning* under the burden of sin without knowing the real reason for their lack of fulfillment and sadness. Some might say with a self-reliant attitude: I'm quite happy without God in my life thank you very much. But those who stop to think seriously about their lives would have to admit sooner or later, that ultimately without God there is no hope for the future—nothing worthwhile to look forward to. Well-known atheists of today such as Richard Dawkins, have expressed their philosophy of life with despairing words such as: We are born, we live, we die, and that's the end of it. However, the biblical truth is, that only when people personally experience the work of the Holy Spirit will they have the opportunity to come into the new life of **"the glorious liberty of the children of God."** How do the unsaved begin to experience the Holy Spirit in order to have a window of opportunity for a new life in Christ? It is by the convicting power that only the Holy Spirit can bring through the witnessing and proclaiming of the truth of the Word of God. Jesus said concerning the Holy Spirit,

"And when He has come, He will convict the world of sin, and of righteousness, and of judgment; of sin, because they do not believe in Me; of righteousness, because I go to My Father and you see Me no more; of judgment, because the ruler of this world is judged" (John 16:8-11).

Since Jesus clearly outlines this work and ministry of the Holy Spirit we could ask: Why are there so many who apparently have absolutely no conviction of wrongdoing as they continue in their lives of sin? For example, never before has American television shown such disrespect for God. Programs are now produced containing material that is nothing less than outright blasphemy and mockery of Christ, the Bible, and everything that is morally good. We are now living in the day and time spoken of by Isaiah the prophet who wrote, **"Woe to those who call evil good, and good evil; who put darkness for light, and light for darkness; who put bitter for sweet, and sweet for bitter!"** (Isaiah 5:20). This happened in Isaiah's day but according to the Apostle Paul things are to get worse before Jesus returns. He wrote, **"But evil men and impostors will grow worse and worse, deceiving and being deceived"** (2 Timothy 3: 13).

Because Satan has been clever enough to influence so many in our day with deceptive ungodly philosophies that keep individuals and groups in spiritual darkness, Christians are being looked upon as hindering and obstructing the so-called advancement of a progressive society. This is how such a worldview can eventually lead to Christians being persecuted, even physically, because we are blocking the so-called *freedom* the ungodly are desperately wanting in order to continue in their sinful immoral lifestyles. There could obviously be a variety of reasons for our culture's downward slide into moral depravity. But today there are more tragedies such as shootings in public places and churches than I can remember compared to the sixties and seventies after I came to America. Today we are seeing literal hatred manifested physically toward Christianity, churches, and almost anything related to the God of the Bible.

We, the Church, have lost our impact on the unsaved public which in the past would normally make them feel ashamed to irreverently attack anything related to God and Christianity. The Church should be a spiritually controlling influence on our society to prevent people from enjoying their sin—which from the Christian point of view is a good thing. In the early days of the Church after God brought judgment on Ananias and his wife for lying to the Holy Spirit we read,

"So great fear come upon all the church and upon all who heard these things." Also, **"And through the hands of the apostles many signs and wonders were done among the people. And they were all with one accord in Solomon's Porch. Yet none of the rest dared join them, but the people esteemed them highly"** (Acts 5:11,12,13).

As representatives of God I believe the Church should be **"esteemed highly"** by the unsaved, but this can only happen when the Church is operating under the awesome power of God the Holy Spirit with evidence of love, holiness and righteous living.

After the Day of Pentecost in the early days of the Church, the Book of Acts gives us the account of a dedicated Christian named Stephen. The testimony given about Stephen reveals he was **"a man full of faith and the Holy Spirit,** and being **"full of faith and power, did great wonders and signs among the people"** (Acts 6:5,8).

From these scriptures we can hardly misunderstand why it was that Stephen had the powerful ministry that his life demonstrated. His obvious effectiveness did not stem from his natural abilities, but there was One dwelling in his spirit who supplied him with the power that flowed through him and from him as he ministered the truth. God the Holy Spirit was working through Stephen in exactly the way Jesus promised His disciples when He had said,

"You shall receive power when the Holy Spirit has come upon you; and you shall be witnesses to Me in Jerusalem, and in all Judea and Samaria, and to the end of the earth" (Acts 1:8).

How was Stephen's witness received? I'm sure it was received with joy by those who were saved, and apparently, many were also miraculously healed along with other signs of God's blessing and presence. When effective ministry and good things like this occur during the proclaiming of the gospel, we can be sure Satan and the wicked spirits of darkness are going to try and hinder the work of God. When this happens we must stand strong in the strength of the Lord, fully trusting Him for what we should say and do, and He will give us the guidance we need. In Stephen's case it was members of the hypocritical religious hierarchy of the day, who were influenced by Satan to oppose him and literally attack him physically. In addition to the urging from the unseen demonic world to attack Stephen, the Holy Spirit was certainly bringing heavy conviction upon these religious leaders. In Acts 7:54 we read, **"When they heard these things they were cut to the heart."** In other words they were powerfully convicted of their wrong standing before God by the presence of the Holy Spirit working through Stephen. Their resistance was so strong to the ministry of Stephen that they completely lost all rationality, and in their demonic rage they literally stoned Stephen to death—the first Christian martyr.

Was this a great victory for Satan? On the surface it would appear so at first, but there was someone present at Stephen's stoning who would soon become a follower of Jesus Christ. This was Paul (or Saul, his Hebrew name), and in the power of the Spirit of God he would be powerfully used of God to plant churches and gain many victories for the Gospel in many geographical areas of his day. I'm sure Paul never forgot his part in the martyrdom of Stephen and other believers he had persecuted before becoming a faithful follower of Jesus Christ himself. Eventually he experienced the same persecution for his faith when he was martyred around A.D. 67 in Rome. His life is a challenging example to us of one who relied on the powerful presence of the living Christ and the Holy Spirit, and who was willing to let the Lord lead him at all costs.

Do American Christians really want to be filled with the presence of God? Because such a life and witness will inevitably invite the attacks of the enemy, to whatever degree the Lord allows. Walking in the power of the Spirit through a dedicated life of seeking the Lord will come at a price. But do Christians know how to seek the Lord for His power today? Do pastors and teachers impress upon those under their preaching and teaching the scriptural importance of obeying the biblical exhortation to **"be filled with the Spirit"**? (Ephesians 5:18). My observation of various ministries reveals that the subject of being filled with the Spirit is something that is not taught or emphasized a great deal, and in fact, may be rarely mentioned. This can be true even in churches and fellowships one would expect to find more emphasis on this subject, such as Pentecostal or charismatic churches. But many other denominational churches don't even mention the subject, and one gets the impression it is assumed that all believers are automatically filled with the Holy Spirit's power. So we need to ask a valid question: Do believers today have the same power and demonstration of the Holy Spirit that the early Church experienced? It is obvious that the answer is: No! Therefore, this leads to asking: If not, why not?

We hear from some parts of the body of Christ that what the early Church experienced is not for us today. We hear that since we have the written Word there is no need for the gifts of the Spirit to be in operation. We hear that the day of miracles is past since the death of the original disciples—with maybe the possibility of a few isolated miracles here and there. We hear that God is sovereign (which is true), and He might occasionally perform miracles today but we have no right to expect such things. Well, if this is true we should mark our Bibles clearly to remind us what sections we can safely believe, and what portions do not apply to us today regarding the supernatural ministry and gifts of the Holy Spirit. Such drastic pruning of the Bible would leave us with a book that is a lot thinner physically and would take less time to read.

I would like to suggest that we should be honest with the Bible and learn about genuine biblical ministry related to the gifts of the Holy Spirit that has taken place in Church history, and in some places is happening today. Many Christians have little or no knowledge of how God has been operating through His Spirit in the Church in supernatural ways, and are not aware of what God is doing in other places around the world. This is generally because they are associated with fellowships that tend to be separatist, self-absorbed and have remained limited to their limited theological genre of approved teaching. But it is surely important as Christians to know what has happened in the past, what is happening today, and what we can trust as reliable information. We sometimes hear skeptics say something silly such as: Prove to me that Jesus Christ even existed! This is as foolish as saying: Prove that George Washington was a real person, or that Napoleon, or Alexander the Great were real people.

What do we need in the way of confirmation about past history in order to believe it? We need two main foundational ingredients: First: Reliable witnesses, and second: Reliable records. This is, of course, exactly what we have in the Bible as well as many secular historical records considered reliable. So, in order to show from comparatively recent recorded history some of the evidence for the power of the Holy Spirit operating in similar ways to the early Church, I will provide the following account of two individuals whose ministry was confirmed by thousands who experienced it. I refer to the gifted evangelists Charles G. Finney and Smith Wigglesworth. First we will look at Finney and the record of his ministry.

Charles Finney (1792-1875) was a passionate and powerful evangelist, who has often been compared to the Great Awakening preachers of the earlier 1700s, Jonathan Edwards, George Whitfield and John Wesley. Thousands were converted under his ministry, and he has been thought of by many as one who was powerfully used to inspire America's second spiritual awakening. A typical example of the effect of Finney's ministry follows when he visited the town of Rochester, New York, in 1830.

Rochester was then a young city, full of new enterprises and full of sin. Finney says the revival swept through the town and changed the great mass of the most influential people, both men and women. This included many physicians and merchants. A large number of leading New York state lawyers lived there, and many were converted. The revival remolded public sentiment, and public affairs came into the hands of Christians with the controlling influence of the community on the side of Christ. Powerful conversions resulted in new leaders who became salt and light for society.

A strange part of the whole story is that Rochester at the time was considered to be 'burnt-over revival territory.' Finney at first had turned down the invitation to come to Rochester, favoring rather invitations to larger cities as New York or Philadelphia. And when he did arrive in Rochester he found religion in a very low state. The churches were suffering from divisions.

It was in the first Rochester revival that Finney introduced the 'anxious seat,' inviting people to come forward to certain front seats 'to a public renunciation of their sinful ways and a public committal of themselves to God.' God gave immediate success to this step, and even the most influential heeded the call.

What brought about all this change? Back of it all was a prevailing spirit of prayer—not only prayer, but a strong and deep *spirit* of prayer, which continued to characterize the whole revival and carry it forward . . . *The spirit of prayer in the churches was the secret.* In that day, as in ours, many were in much darkness with regard to this greater praying. Finney says, 'There must be in the church a deeper sense of the need of the spirit of prayer.' It is not that our congregations are prayerless, but so seldom do we find a church *with the spirit of prayer resting on the congregation.* That is what is missing; that is what must come back. That is the revival we need. (Charles G. Finney, *Power From on High.* Preface by Armin R. Gesswein, 1984 vii-ix).

To what did Finney attribute his powerful spiritual influence over those he ministered to wherever he went? As emphasized above, it was an increase in the spirit of prayer. It was not just the regular prayers prayed in meetings, but a spirit of prayer that drew Christians into a deeper commitment to earnest prayer that caused it to become a priority in their daily lives. Did something supernatural happen to Finney that propelled him forward into his life's occupation as a minister of the Gospel? In the following excerpt, Finney recounts his empowering by the Holy Spirit while alone in his law office after his conversion in the autumn of 1821. From his (***Memoirs of Rev. Charles G. Finney.*** New York: A.S. Barnes & Co., 1876 20-21).

"But as I turned and was about to take a seat by the fire, I received a mighty baptism of the Holy Ghost. Without any expectation of it, without ever having the thought in my mind that there was any such thing for me, without my recollection that I had ever heard the thing mentioned by any person in the world, the Holy Ghost descended on me in a manner that seemed to go through me, body and soul. I could feel the impression, like a wave of electricity, going through and through me. Indeed it seemed to come in waves and waves of liquid love; for I could not express it in any other way. It seemed like the very breath of God. I can recollect distinctly that it seemed to fan me, like immense wings.

No words can express the wonderful love that was shed abroad in my heart. I wept aloud with joy and love; and I do not know but I should say, I literally bellowed out the unutterable gushings of my heart. The waves came over me, and over me, one after the other, until I recollect I cried out, "I shall die if these waves continue to pass over me." I said, "Lord, I cannot bear any more"; yet I had no fear of death.

How long I continued in this state, with this baptism continuing to roll over me and go through me, I do not know. But I know it was late in the evening when a member of my choir—for I was the leader of the choir—came into the office to see me in this state of loud weeping, and said to me, "Mr. Finney, what ails you?" I could make him no answer for some time. He then said, "Are you in pain?" I gathered myself up as best I could, and replied, "No, but so happy that I cannot live."

He turned and left the office, and in a few minutes returned with one of the elders of the church, whose shop was nearly across the way from our office. This elder was a very serious man; and in my presence had been very watchful, and I had scarcely ever seen him laugh. When he came in, I was very much in the state in which I was when the young man went out to call him. He asked me how I felt, and I began to tell him. Instead of saying anything, he fell into a most spasmodic laughter. It seemed as if it was impossible for him to keep from laughing from the very bottom of his heart."

This is what Finney experienced in 1821 which thrust

him into the ministry until his life ended in 1875. In his later years Finney wrote,

> "Personal fellowship with God is the secret of the whole of it . . . I have infinitely more hope for the usefulness of a man who, at any cost, will keep up daily fellowship with God; who is yearning for and struggling after the highest possible spiritual attainment; who will not live without daily prevalence in prayer and being clothed with power from on high . . . I beg the seminaries, to receive a word of exhortation from an old man, who has had some experience in these things, and one whose heart mourns and is weighed down in view of the shortcomings of the Church, the ministers, and the seminaries on this subject. Brethren, I beseech you to more thoroughly consider this matter, to wake up and lay it to heart, and rest not until this subject of the **enduement of power** from on high is brought forward into its proper place and takes that prominent position in the view of the whole Church that Christ intended it should" (Charles G. Finney. *Power From on High*. Christian Literature Crusade, Pennsylvania, 1984 38-40 *emphasis mine*).

Obviously, Finney recounts a dramatic experience with the Holy Spirit that many Christians do not identify with today. But was Finney's experience any more dramatic than that of the early believers (about 120 people, Acts 1:15) on the Day of Pentecost when they were so exhilarated after the Holy Spirit descended upon them that we read, **"Others mocking said, 'They are full of new wine'"** (Acts 2:13). The Apostle Peter soon corrected this accusation by saying, **"For these are not drunk, as you suppose, since it is *only* the third hour of the day"** (Acts 2:15). Apparently there were physical manifestations that encouraged this accusation. The point of all this is that Christians need the powerful presence of the Holy Spirit in their lives in order to be the most effective witnesses for the Lord. If we have not been taught to ask for, wait for, believe and have faith for His power it is doubtful we will ever experience such blessing and enduement.

You may remember the experience I shared in chapter ten which totally transformed my life and gave me boldness to witness. Different people will probably have differing experiences, for God knows exactly what we need as individuals. However, I believe we should all seek for the fullness of the Holy Spirit in our lives so we can be all that God has planned for us to be. Next we will look at another widely known evangelist who ministered in the power of the Spirit in his day. Smith Wigglesworth, is one who has been referred to by many as a true *apostle of faith*.

Who could have ever predicted that an uneducated plumber from Bradford, England, would ever be used by God in a worldwide ministry? Born in 1859, Smith Wigglesworth was converted at the age of eight in a Wesleyan Methodist meeting. As a teenager he developed a zeal to see others become Christians and worked with the Salvation Army for a few years. He also spent time ministering to many poverty stricken children in the Liverpool boat dock areas where hundreds were saved. Returning to Bradford he opened his own plumbing business. He married Polly Featherstone who was a dynamic soul winner, and joined her in her work at a small gospel mission in Bradford.

In 1907 at the age of 48 Wigglesworth's life entered a new phase. He began to receive calls to minister from many countries around the world, and through his huge meetings he led thousands to faith in Jesus Christ.

His faith-filled messages and ministry brought healing and deliverance to untold numbers. It should remind us of the Stephen we read about in the Book of Acts which reads, **"And Stephen, full of faith and power, did great wonders and signs among the people"** (Acts 6:8). Wigglesworth's ministry also reminds us of Philip, the deacon and evangelist of whom we read,

"Then Philip went down to the city of Samaria and preached Christ to them. And the multitudes with one accord heeded the things spoken by Philip, hearing and seeing the miracles which he did. For unclean spirits, crying with a loud voice, came out of many who were possessed; and many who were paralyzed and lame were healed" (Acts 8:5-7).

Wigglesworth spoke in a down-to-earth way about how a Christian can minister with the power of God. He said,

> "None of you can be strong in God unless you diligently hearken to what God has to say to you through His Word. You cannot know the power and the nature of God unless you partake of His inbreathed Word.
>
> Read it at morn and at night and at every opportunity you get. After every meal, instead of indulging in unprofitable conversation round the table, read a chapter from the Word and then have a season of prayer.
>
> I endeavor to make a point of doing this no matter where or with whom I am staying . . . as you receive God's Word into your being, your whole physical being will be quickened and you will be made strong. As you receive with meekness the Word, you will find faith springing up within. And

you will have life through the Word" (Smith Wigglesworth. *Ever Increasing Faith,* Gospel Publishing House, Springfield, Missouri, 1971 102,103).

People who knew Wigglesworth and spent time with him, testified that this is truly the way he lived for many years as he ministered in different countries around the world. Thousands were saved, healed, and delivered through his ministry. Here's an example of his one-on-one ministry recorded in shorthand as he was preaching,

> A man came to me one time, brought by a little woman. I said, "What's up with him?" [Wigglesworth's way of asking about a person's need] She said, "He gets situations [work], but he fails every time. He is a slave to alcohol and nicotine poison. He is a bright, intelligent man in most things, but he goes under to those two things." I was reminded of the words of the Master, giving us power to bind and loose, and I told him to put out his tongue. In the name of the Lord Jesus Christ I cast out the evil powers that gave him the taste for these things. I said to him, "Man, you are free today." He was unsaved, but when he realized the power of the Lord in delivering him, he came to the services, publicly acknowledged that he was a sinner, and the Lord saved and baptized him. A few days later I asked, "How are things with you?" He said, "I am delivered" (Smith Wigglesworth. *Faith That Prevails.* Gospel Publishing House, Springfield, Missouri. 1966 22,23).

Yes, Wigglesworth was certainly an enigma to the conservative Christian theologians of his day, but none could deny the power he had with God and the thousands who testified to salvation and healing. Here is another typical report from his ministry,

> HEALINGS IN NEW ZEALAND: We have received a few testimonies of those healed in the meeting conducted by Brother Smith Wigglesworth at Wellington, New Zealand. Mrs. E. Curtis of Christchurch, New Zealand, was suffering with septic poisoning. She had become only a skeleton and the doctors could do nothing for her. She had agonizing pains all day and all night. She was healed immediately when prayer was made for her. She states that for the past sixteen years she has been a martyr to pain but is now wonderfully well.
>
> Another testified to healing of double curvature of the spine from infancy, hip disease, weak heart, leg lengthened three inches, which grew normal like the other leg. It was also three inches less in circumference. She wore a large boot but now walks on even feet, the large boot having been discarded. Another was healed from goiter.—*The Pentecostal Evangel* (Smith Wigglesworth. *Ever Increasing Faith*. Gospel Publishing House, Springfield, Missouri. 1971 16).

We see from these sample accounts the evidence that the Holy Spirit's power can operate through believers today in similar ways to that of the early Church. That is, if God's people will truly seek the Lord and believe in simple child-like faith. Jesus said, **"He who abides in Me, and I in him, bears much fruit; for without Me you can do nothing"** (John 15:5). He also said, **"But you shall receive power when the Holy Spirit has come upon you; and you shall be witnesses to Me"** (Acts 1:8). We must come to the place of faith in our minds and hearts to know our witness must be by His power from within us. On a personal note, I know that any witness of mine that results in something of eternal value, will only be by *His power, not mine.*

CHAPTER 14

HIS WORD WILL PREVAIL

Words, words, words! What an amazing gift God has given the zenith of His creation—us. We are the only ones with the inherent gifting of having conscious thoughts in our minds, which we can then speak out in a language for others to understand. Some have claimed, and I believe rightly so, that we are the only beings on earth able to *think about thinking!* Because we have this gift of speech, which is partly due to our unique vocal chords, humans have learned to put words into writing.

This is evidenced from architectural discoveries dating back at least four to five thousand years or beyond. In fact, I believe in the possibility of God's first human, Adam, being able to put his thoughts into writing. He lived for 930 years with an almost perfect body and brilliant intelligence—for example, he named many of the animals which was an amazing feat in itself.

During those long years of life it is more than feasible he would have been able to figure out how to record his thoughts and knowledge on something tangible, such as cuneiform clay tablets. For example, today's archeologists believe early forms of intelligent writing as discovered on clay tablets were invented by the Sumerians in Mesopotamia around 3,200 B.C. or beyond. Interestingly, this suggests the possibility that Adam was still living if the Genesis creation event took place approximately 6,000 years ago—as indicated by the biblical genealogies.

LEFT: One of the Syrian tablets from Elba known as creation tablets, because one of them referred to the fact that there was no Heaven, and Lugal ("The Great One") formed It out of nothing.

Photo by Rod Butterworth

If I had been Adam I'm sure I would have been curious about the basic questions of life; who am I, where did I come from, and why am I here? It would seem that God must have answered Adam's questions personally. This would most likely have been during the times they spent together in the Garden of Eden before the tragic entrance of sin into the world. Although we cannot prove it, it is possible that physical records made by Adam could have found their way into the hands of Noah, and even Moses. Orally rehearsed history is also a likely possibility.

With this little summary about the history of words, we now consider the most important of all words, God's words. In our creation museum one of the first things visitors see is a sign which says, *The History Book of the Universe* with a picture of the Bible included. Without the Bible, no other religious book makes sense of the world and universe we live in. Why is this so? Because it is *God's Word!* It is the Word of the almighty God of all creation who is the giver of life. He knows the answers to our questions.

How sad that many have rejected God's Word because they are not willing to admit their need to humble themselves, and come into fellowship with God on His terms. This is the way things got off to a wrong start in the garden when Adam and Eve took things into their own hands, and rebelled in disobedience to *God's terms.* Yes, Satan's presence was allowed by God to see if Adam and Eve would pass the test—otherwise God would be an absolute arbitrary dictator which is not His nature as revealed in the Scriptures. God did not create us to be like puppets on strings with no independent choices of free will permitted. But unfortunately they failed the test, and death entered the world which changed everything (Romans 5:12). They failed to give priority to the words God had spoken to them, and tragically, their fellowship with God was broken leading to their immediate expulsion from the garden never to return. Jesus warned concerning the absolute importance of us giving His words the supreme authority, obedience and respect they require when He said,

"Do not think that I came to destroy the Law or the Prophets. I did not come to destroy but to fulfill. For assuredly, I say to you, till heaven and earth pass away, one jot [Hebrew *yod,* smallest letter] **or one tittle** [smallest stroke in a Hebrew letter] **will by no means pass from the law till all is fulfilled.**

Whoever therefore breaks one of the least of these commandments, and teaches men so, shall be called least in the kingdom of heaven; but whoever does and teaches *them,* **he shall be called great in the kingdom of heaven"** (Matthew 5:17-19).

Proverbs 30:5,6 also cautions us concerning our treatment of God's Word where we read, **"Every word of God** *is* **pure; He is a shield to those who put their trust in Him. Do not add to His words, lest He rebuke you, and you be found a liar."** Words are powerful, but none more so than God's words. The Bible says, **"Death and life** *are* **in the power of the tongue, and those who love it will eat its fruit"** (Proverbs 18:21).

Think about this for a moment. Spiritually you are either projecting life or death to those around you. This primarily depends on how you use your tongue. We should seriously consider before God the eternal import of our interaction with others when we use this wonderful gift of speech. The Bible also says, **"But I say to you that for every idle word men may speak, they will give account of it in the day of judgment"** (Matthew 12:36). Jesus obviously took the gift of speech and the words we use very seriously. Our words will definitely have eternal consequences.

How does all this relate to the need for revival in America? It has to do with the words we use when we pray. What kind of words would God want us to use when we pray for revival or any other petitions and desires we may have in our hearts? I see clearly from Scripture that He wants us to use words of faith—specifically, words of faith without doubting in our hearts. Jesus taught His disciples about prayer through words and by example. In a passage of what is generally referred to as the Lord's Prayer, Jesus instructs us to pray with the words, **"Your will be done on earth as *it is* in heaven"** (Matthew 6:10). This implies that believers should recognize the need to submit to God's will, both concerning what it is they are praying for as well as that which concerns their individual lives. This in turn implies that the words of our prayers need to be in line with God's will. If we are sincere when we pray we will desire God's will to **"be done on earth"** *in us,* so we will be all that God wants us to be. Of course, what God's plan is for us to be and to become will always be the best for us.

So what is His will for the unsaved in America—how should we pray for them? The most basic need would obviously be for them to be saved. And what is His will for His Church in America? Obviously that the body of Christ will be spiritually alive with a dynamic relationship with Him individually and corporately. And what is His will for each of us individually who claim to be part of His spiritual body? It is to totally surrender our wills and desires to Him with a commitment to love and serve Him above all others.

In order for us to move ahead in revival and the will of God we must build upon a solid foundation. There is no better foundation for building up the kingdom of God and our individual lives than the living Word of God applied to us by the Holy Spirit. Jesus said, **"It is the Spirit who gives life; the flesh profits nothing. The words that I speak to you are spirit, and *they* are life"** (John 6:63). We may not hear audible words from the Lord today, but His words as faithfully recorded in the New Testament are just as full of His life as when He spoke them. The question is: Will we come before Him humbly so the Holy Spirit will cause His words to come alive to us and within us? Following is a listing of scriptures that will encourage us in our prayer life for revival to impact America. I suggest reading them slowly and prayerfully.

"For we *were* slaves. Yet our God did not forsake us in our bondage; but He extended mercy to us in the sight of the kings of Persia, to revive us, to repair the house of our God, to rebuild its ruins, and to give us a wall in Judah and Jerusalem" (Ezra 9:9).

And he spoke before his brethren and the army of Samaria, and said, "What are these feeble Jews doing? Will they fortify themselves? Will they offer sacrifices? Will they complete it in a day? Will they revive the stones from the heaps of rubbish—*stones* that are burned?" (Nehemiah 4:2).

"*You,* who have shown me great and severe troubles, shall revive me again, and bring me up

again from the depths of the earth" (Psalm 71:20).

"Then we will not turn back from You; Revive us, and we will call upon Your name" (Psalm 80:18).

"Will You not revive us again, that Your people may rejoice in You?" (Psalm 85:6).

"My soul clings to the dust; revive me according to Your word" (Psalm 119:25).

"Turn away my eyes from looking at worthless things, *and* revive me in Your way" (Psalm 119:37).

"Behold, I long for Your precepts; revive me in Your righteousness" (Psalm 119:40).

"Revive me according to Your lovingkindness, so that I may keep the testimony of Your mouth" (Psalm 119:88).

"I am afflicted very much; revive me, O LORD, according to Your word" Psalm 119:107).

"Hear my voice according to Your lovingkindness; O LORD, revive me according to Your justice" (Psalm 119:149).

"Plead my cause and redeem me; revive me according to Your word" (Psalm 119:154).

"Great *are* Your tender mercies, O LORD; revive me according to Your judgments" (Psalm 119:56).

"Consider how I love Your precepts; revive me, O LORD, according to Your lovingkindness" (Psalm 119:159).

"Though I walk in the midst of trouble, You will revive me; You will stretch out Your hand against the wrath of my enemies, and Your right hand will save me" (Psalm 138:7).

"Revive me, O LORD, for Your name's sake! For Your righteousness' sake bring my soul out of trouble" (Psalm 143:11).

For thus says the High and Lofty One Who inhabits eternity, whose name *is* Holy: "I dwell in the high and holy *place,* with him *who* has a contrite and humble spirit, to revive the spirit of the humble, and to revive the heart of the contrite ones (Isaiah 57:15).

"Those who dwell under his shadow shall return; they shall be revived *like* grain, and grow like a vine. Their scent *shall be* like the wine of Lebanon" (Hosea 14:7).

"O LORD, I have heard Your speech *and* was afraid; O LORD, revive Your work in the midst of the years! In the midst of the years make *it* known; in wrath remember mercy" (Habakkuk 3:2).

"Repent therefore and be converted, that your sins may be blotted out, so that times of refreshing may come from the presence of the Lord" (Acts 3:19).

"But those who wait on the LORD shall renew *their* strength; they shall mount up with wings like eagles, they shall run and not be weary, they shall walk and not faint" (Isaiah 40:31).

"Create in me a clean heart, O God, and renew a steadfast spirit within me" (Psalm 51:10).

"Turn us back to You, O LORD, and we will be

restored; renew our days as of old"** (Lamentations 5:21).

"Therefore strengthen the hands which hang down, and the feeble knees" (Hebrews 12:12).

"Therefore we do not lose heart. Even though our outward *man* is perishing, yet the inward man is being renewed day by day" (2 Corinthians 4:16).

I will now repeat the first scripture on the above list, because I believe there is a parallel to the situation we are facing in America today.

"For we *were* slaves. Yet our God did not forsake us in our bondage; but He extended mercy to us in the sight of the kings of Persia, to revive us, to repair the house of our God, to rebuild its ruins, and to give us a wall in Judah and Jerusalem" (Ezra 9:9).

The truth is we were all slaves to sin until God rescued us by His grace and love through the Gospel. Now we see multitudes of Americans who are slaves to sin, and most of them don't even realize what is happening to them as they stumble through life without knowledge of ultimate meaning. Obviously, living in a society where so many people do not know God, affects us as Christians in ways that makes us sad and uncomfortable—at least, it should if we have any sense of the heart of God.

So if we are concerned about the spiritual **"bondage"** around us, we can have assurance that if we pray and seek the Lord as we should then He will **"not forsake us."** Psalm 100:5 says, **"For the Lord is good; His mercy *is* everlasting, and His truth** [or faithfulness] ***endures* to all generations."** Yes, He can bring revival to the millions in our country who are presently walking in spiritual darkness. If we truly believe in our great God and pray with fasting and persevering faith, we can see Him move by the power of His Spirit **"to revive us"** and, **"to repair the house of our God"** and, **"to rebuild its ruins"** and, **"to give us a wall"** of protection for the Church to stand strong against Satan and all the enemies of God.

Jesus clearly wants us to pray for revival of His people with the kind of determined attitude that indicates we will not take no for an answer. Of course, it should go without saying that our petitions must be within the boundary of God's sovereign will and purposes, and His Word is our God-given guide to give us confidence to ask according to His will. After Jesus gave His disciples a guide for daily prayer—usually referred to as the Lord's Prayer—He encouraged them to be consistent and not become discouraged. We find two illustrations in the gospels where Jesus emphasized the need for faithful, continuing, and persevering prayer.

First, Jesus painted a picture of a man who had a surprise visitor and had no bread to provide sustenance and hospitality for his guest. He went to his friend's house to ask for a loan of bread, but it was at the midnight hour. His friend said he could not give him the bread because he and his family were already in bed. At this point in the story Jesus says,

"I say to you, though he will not rise and give him because he is his friend, yet because of his persistence he will rise and give him as many as he needs. So I say to you, ask, and it will be given to you; seek, and you will find; knock, and it will be opened to you.

For everyone who asks receives, and he who seeks finds, and to him who knocks it will be

opened . . .how much more will *your* heavenly Father give the Holy Spirit [in revival] **to those who ask Him!"** (Luke 11:8-10,13).

What remains for us to do is simply to put into practice this kind of faith and persistence as we come to the Lord in prayer with our requests. The promises and encouragement are there for us in the Bible, but will we really believe the words of our Lord? The second illustration Jesus gave for the same purpose is a parable found in Luke 18:1-8.

Then He spoke a parable to them, that men always ought to pray and not lose heart, saying: "There was in a certain city a judge who did not fear God nor regard man. Now there was a widow in that city; and she came to him, saying, 'Get justice for me from my adversary.' And he would not for a while; but afterward he said within himself, 'Though I do not fear God nor regard man, yet because this widow troubles me I will avenge her, lest by her continual coming she weary me.'"

Then the Lord said, "Hear what the unjust judge said. And shall God not avenge His own elect who cry out day and night to Him, though He bears long with them? I tell you that He will avenge them speedily. Nevertheless, when the Son of Man comes, will He really find faith on the earth?"

I believe the most important part of this parable of Jesus is seen in the last clause. It is a challenge from Jesus. He asks whether He will find the kind of faith He is looking for in His followers when He returns at His second coming. What kind of faith is He looking for? Faith that harbors no doubts that the Word of God and the promises it contains are absolutely reliable, authentic, trustworthy, dependable, and true. After all, the Word of God as recorded in our printed Bibles is backed up by the

One who is, **"The Way, the truth, and the life"** (John 14:6). Jesus told the parable above for the very specific purpose, **"that men ought always to pray and not lose heart."**

As recorded in the Book of Acts chapter twelve, what were the early Christians doing while Peter was imprisoned in Jerusalem and facing certain death? Stephen had already been stoned, and James the brother of John had been executed by King Herod. Now it looked as though the Church was about to see Peter suffer the same fate. Things looked extremely discouraging from a human point of view. But in Acts 12:5 we read, **"Peter was therefore kept in prison, but constant** [Gr. *ektenos* fervent, earnest] **prayer was offered to God for him by the church."** Those early believers did not retreat with a fatalistic attitude and do nothing. They did not lose heart because they knew the teaching of Jesus about having faith and not giving up when the situation looked hopeless. After all, Jesus had said, **"If you abide in Me, and My words abide in you, you will ask what you desire, and it shall be done for you"** (John 15:7). And, **"If you can believe, all things are possible to him who believes"** (Mark 9:23).

At the beginning of the paragraph above I asked: What were the early Christians doing while Peter was imprisoned in Jerusalem and was facing certain death? Now I ask my brothers and sisters in Christ across this beloved land a pointed question: What are *we* doing while the America we have known in the past is currently being destroyed before our very eyes? What are we doing to counteract the attacks on the biblical values upon which this nation was founded? Have we been blindsided by the enemy to the extent that we don't realize the reality of the battle that is staring us in the face? It is one thing just to know the situation, but another to be actively engaged in the drama of the outcome, and to actually have a part in affecting the outcome. Those early Christians obviously believed in the reality and power of the words of Jesus. This kept them praying fervently into the dead of night for Peter's life to be spared. Some of them may have found it very hard to believe Peter could be spared from death. But faith and prayer in the words of Jesus prevailed, and Peter was miraculously delivered from the powers of darkness. It was a victory over the influence of Satan and evil spirits who were the real enemies behind Herod's murderous intentions.

It is surely necessary for all of us to take inventory of the words we use every day in our conversations with others, and especially in our prayers to God. We should take to heart seriously the words of Jesus when He said, **"For by your words you will be justified, and by your words you will be condemned"** (Matthew 12:37).

Faith, prayer, and the Word combined together as we make our requests to God are powerful weapons available to all of us, if only we will use them. Our speech should be full of words of faith, not doubt, unbelief or negativity. Yes, be sure to believe in the amazing promises in God's Word as you pray for revival, the renewal of the Church, and the salvation of the lost. Remember, His Word will prevail.

CHAPTER 15

THE POWER OF LIVING IN HIS LOVE

We cannot escape them; the two greatest commandments ever given to us by God:

"You shall love the Lord your God with all your heart, with all your soul, and with all your mind. This is the first and great commandment.

And the second is like it: You shall love your neighbor as yourself. On these two commandments hang all the Law and the Prophets" (Matthew 22:37-40).

If we want to see a revival move of God across America we will only see it if we obey these two commandments. The quality of unconditional love of God and neighbor should be so strong though our lives as believers and the Church as a whole, that this by itself will be a tremendous witness to the truth of the gospel. However, if we live our lives selfishly with no concern for the eternal spiritual welfare of our neighbors, we would do well to examine ourselves as to whether we are **"in the faith"** (2 Corinthians 13:5). Jesus prayed for twenty-first-century Christians and is still praying for us today. He said,

"I do not pray for these alone, but also for those who will believe in Me through their word [that's us!]**; that they all may be one, as You, Father, *are* in Me, and I in You; that they also may be one in Us, that the world may believe that You sent Me"** (John 17:20,21).

Without this love of God within us which produces

love for one another, we will not see revival. Jesus desires us to be one in unity with Himself and the Father, **"that they also may be one in Us."** If we are in truth walking through the days of our Christian lives with the wonderful personal relationship with Him He wants us to have, we should increasingly love others as He does. Of course, God loves all of humanity and is, **"not willing that any should perish but that all should come to repentance"** (2 Peter 3:9).

As I write about this wonderful subject of love I am observing our nation in turmoil. People are expressing hatred and brutality across America in ways that the Bible has predicted would take place during the last period of history before the Lord returns. This type of cultural degeneration is what happens when the influence of the gospel is weak. Paul wrote about those who would increasingly produce evil through their words and actions. People would be, **"unloving, unforgiving, slanderers, without self-control, brutal, despisers of good, traitors, headstrong, haughty, lovers of pleasure rather than lovers of God"** (2 Timothy 3:3,4).

An example of this scripture was seen in yet another senseless shooting in October, 2017, which killed over 60 with over 500 injured after a gunman shot into a large crowd attending an outdoor concert in Las Vegas, Nevada. There seems to be a madness in the air. Well, there certainly is a madness in the spiritual air and it is encouraged by demonic influence. Paul writes about the reality of spiritual warfare with these words,

"Finally, my brethren, be strong in the Lord and in the power of His might. Put on the whole armor of God, that you may be able to stand against the wiles of the devil. For we do not wrestle against flesh and blood, but against principalities, against

powers, against the rulers of the darkness of this age, against spiritual *hosts* **of wickedness in the heavenly** *places* [or, heavenlies]" (Ephesians 6:10-12).

It is not just political change that is causing such unrest, although this obviously can be a significant factor. But the reason for the open hatred, violent protests and hateful vitriolic language runs much deeper than mere political disagreement. The Bible asks, **"Can two walk together, unless they are agreed?** (Amos 3:3). The answer is, of course not! We Christians must actively stand strong with faith in the words of Jesus and the powerful promise He gave us, **"Behold, I give you the authority to trample on serpents and scorpions, and over all the power of the enemy, and nothing shall by any means hurt you"** (Luke 10:19). We must stand strong in the authority Jesus has given us as we engage in this spiritual warfare, and it is vital that we do engage.

A huge divide has developed in America today that separates the hearts and minds of people from one another and pulls them in opposite directions. One way to describe it is to realize the increase of underlying opposing different *worldviews,* which are deeply embedded in the thinking of so many. The clash of these worldviews has become so strong, that humanly speaking there would seemingly be little hope of a coming together in agreement.

A worldview is an accumulation of life experiences gained from culture, family, friends, teachers, and education in general. For example, if you were raised in India as a member of a Hindu family, your worldview would most likely include the belief that the Hindu religion is the correct one and Indian culture is the best in the world. On meeting someone of a different religious belief you would not feel comfortable or at ease with them because they would have a different worldview. The Christian worldview would be belief that the Bible is the Word of God as opposed to the belief that it is not. Such opposing views can never be resolved until one side is willing to search for truth with an open, humble and transparent attitude. Christians do have an advantage, because through believing prayer we have seen many do a complete turnaround of their beliefs. This can happen when they are willing to let the Holy Spirit lead them into truth.

In our creation museum ministry we come across the problem of differing worldviews on a regular basis. We teach that evolution—the kind Darwin thought would cause one living creature to change over time into a completely new and different creature (macro-evolution)—is not true, because it is not scientifically supported. However, millions of young people have been taught in our secular educational institutions that Darwin's idea of evolution is true.

So what is the solution? We have to gently speak the truth in love (Ephesians 4:15), and pray that the Holy Spirit will give them a window of opportunity to be willing to examine the actual scientific evidence with an open mind. We have learned the hard way that no one ever wins an argument except in their own mind. But how should we deal with those who express personal hatred to us because of opposing worldviews—as for example, what we see in prolife verses pro-abortion encounters? Again, we must pray for the Holy Spirit to give us wisdom and boldness to speak the truth in love.

Yes, loving our neighbor is no easy task. In fact, on the human level it can seem impossible to us as we rub shoulders with certain people and experience personality conflicts with them. It is interesting that in recent times atheists have said they are free to make their own good moral decisions, without any interaction or involvement with a god. But those who claim they can be good and love others without God, have missed the reason why they cannot generate real genuine spiritual-level love from the heart, which is because they are trying to do it mentally at the surface level. However, if someone was trying to kill them I don't think they would normally be willing to express love to that person.

Atheist/comedian Bill Maher has said with a typical misunderstanding of God's love and of who God is, "Let's face it; God has a big ego problem. Why do we have to worship him?" (www.brainyquote.com, accessed 10-1-2017). I would answer this by reminding him that we love and worship God because He loved us first when we did not deserve it, and sacrificed His life on the cross in order for us to have a loving relationship with Him. We have all heard expressions concerning young children such as, "She adores her daddy." When we express our love and worship to God we are like young children adoring their parents, because without them we would be missing the advantage of their wisdom and the benefit of the security they offer.

In like manner we should recognize that we desperately need our wonderful Creator. God is omnipotent (all powerful), He created the universe, omniscient (all knowing), and omnipresent (everywhere present by His Spirit), and we are as less than infants in comparison. God is too big to have an ego problem! Yet, God created us to have a personal relationship with Him and this is the greatest desire of His heart. It is therefore absolutely right that we should love and worship Him.

Because of the love we experience from God as we put faith in Him, there are many examples of the power of love seen in the lives of His followers. Unlike atheists who would not be expected to love someone who was trying to kill them, there are believers in Jesus Christ who have literally demonstrated genuine love in similar situations. After the Day of Pentecost when the Church was beginning to be formed, Stephen (mentioned earlier) was one of the early disciples who was radical in his zeal and willingness to stand up for the truth.

He spoke boldly with the convicting power of the Holy Spirit to the religious leaders who were opposing him. He wanted them to come into the same relationship with God he had discovered. He was literally willing to risk his life for the truth about Jesus. He was a radical witness for the resurrection of Christ. What happened as Stephen continued speaking shows that he must have had genuine concern for his hearers, even love for them. They were convicted by the Holy Spirit but would not humble themselves and confess their guilt and blindness, so they stoned Stephen to death. However, just before he lost consciousness he prayed for his persecutors with these words, **"Lord, do not charge them with this sin"** (Acts 7:60).

Why was Stephen able to love his neighbor as himself at the very moment he was being violently murdered? It was because he had something within—the presence of Jesus and the Holy Spirit—motivating him at a level of love far deeper than that which would be only of surface level. He had found out by experience the wonderful truth, that by loving God first he was then able to love others because the love of God was in his heart.

The Apostle Paul wrote, **"Now hope does not disappoint, because the love of God has been poured out in our hearts by the Holy Spirit who was given to us"** (Romans 5:5). The promise of God is given to all of us as believers, and is available to us as we ask in faith for the fullness of God's love to permeate our own hearts. If we do not feel we are manifesting God's love as we should, it is time to press into a more intimate relationship with Him. This can only come about through prayer and meditation in His Word until our lives are overflowing with genuine love for God and others.

Returning to John 17 and the prayer of Jesus when He prayed, **"that the world may believe that You sent Me"** (verse 21), we can understand the ultimate purpose for developing an intimate loving relationship with God, and a true love for our neighbor. It is to convince the unsaved in the reality of Jesus Christ, who He is, and what He has done for us by His death, burial, and resurrection. It is to see the Holy Spirit move upon the unsaved by bringing them to salvation.

Jesus is still interceding for us today that this would be the effect of our relationship with Him. In other words, if our lives are overflowing with the love of God because of our intimate relationship with Him, our witness can be the stimulus and cause for others to believe in Him. This is revival in the making! If it is true that the pendulum of American population has swung to the side of the unsaved being more numerous than the saved, we can see it swing back the other way if we will obey God according to the two Great Commandments.

One of the greatest scriptural challenges for testing our degree of love for God and others is found in First Corinthians chapter thirteen. I sometimes ask God to tread on my toes if there are areas of my life which need correction. Thank God, He does it gently or I might be devastated by such revelations. One of the subjects where I feel a constant need for improvement is this one, love. There will be no change in communities for the better without an atmosphere and demonstration of genuine love. The first three verses of this chapter read:

"Though I speak with the tongues of men and of angels, but have not love, I have become

sounding brass or a clanging cymbal. And though I have *the gift* of prophecy, and understand all mysteries and all knowledge, and though I have all faith, so that I could remove mountains, but have not love, I am nothing. And though I bestow all my goods to feed *the* poor, and though I give my body to be burned, but have not love, it profits me nothing."

We may be blest with spiritual gifts and have deep understanding with knowledge about mysteries more than others, but we will be missing God's main purpose for us if we don't operate in the purity of God's love. Unfortunately, it seems to be a predominant misunderstanding people have about their outward altruistic acts of service to others, that these things by themselves are gaining the approval of God. But it is the underlying motive that God is looking for, and by the way, He always knows the underlying motive! So when we give to God's work and feel pretty good about it, let's not fall into the trap of mentally patting ourselves on the back with the inward thought: I must be pleasing to God. But what of the motive? We must always consider our motives. Without the motive of love these things will ultimately profit us **"nothing."** However, if done because the love of God is leading and guiding us, such ministry will reap eternal rewards, and perhaps revival. Verse four reads:

"Love suffers long *and* is kind; love does not envy; love does not parade itself, is not puffed up [or, arrogant]."

I had a dear Christian friend for many years who is now in heaven. His wife suffered a high fever at midlife that left her unable to function normally. She had to be looked after at a care center and was a resident there for eleven years. For the entire eleven years her husband, though busy with his business, visited her every day while remaining faithful to his wedding vows. This was a wonderful example to me of what it means to suffer long and be kind. I would sadly have to admit that he was probably one of a minority who would do what he did so faithfully. What about the subject of envy? A test of this would be when our neighbor is blest with prosperity and advantage which we do not experience ourselves. Are we genuinely happy when our neighbor is blest? We should be glad and rejoice with him. If we cannot do this it points to our need for a time on our knees until we have the right perspective, or we may be hindering the spirit of revival.

When we do receive blessing from God we should not make the mistake of boasting about it in an arrogant way. The best way to handle God's blessings upon us is to first of all thank God with genuine thankfulness every time the subject comes up in conversation with others. Let us also be careful when talking about revivals when they come into our midst. The temptation to exaggerate, which is a form of boasting, can help dampen the fires of revival. In the creation museum ministry in which I am involved we have seen God bless us in marvelous ways that were totally unexpected—except that we were praying for God's help and the answer came. Can we take any credit for such because we were praying? Absolutely not! It is all God's doing. Our prayers were just a part of our cooperation and willingness to pray and trust God, and He was gracious enough to answer our prayers. The very fact that we can pray and our prayers reach God is because of His love, grace, and the fact that our wonderful mediator, Jesus, is interceding for us. To Him be the thanks, the glory and the praise. May we experience the power of living in His love.

CHAPTER 16

REVIVAL THROUGH RELATIONSHIP

How close do you think your relationship with the Lord is today? You may say: Well, I know I'm saved, so I guess my relationship with the Lord is OK. Another penetrating question: Do you believe you are living in a state of personal spiritual revival today? This is a very intimate question and would obviously be answered in a number of different ways by different people. So how do Christians become spiritually revived, and how would we know if we are in a state of spiritual revival or not? We need to go back to a scripture we have mentioned a few times earlier in this book where we are exhorted by the Apostle Paul to do something I believe is of great importance. He wrote,

"Examine yourselves *as to* whether you are in the faith. Test yourselves. Do you not know yourselves, that Jesus Christ is in you?—unless indeed you are disqualified" (2 Corinthians 13:5).

How do we examine ourselves? How do we test ourselves? First of all we must be prepared to be totally honest and transparent as we come before the Lord. In order to prepare personally for this I find it almost essential to be alone and quiet in His presence without distractions. There is something special and intimate about being alone with God in a peaceful and quiet environment. The Bible says, **"Be still, and know that I *am* God"** (Psalm 46:10). Also, **"Meditate within your heart on your bed, and be still"** (Psalm 4:4). And we should not forget the example of Jesus who carefully prioritized his time, **"And when He had sent the multitudes away, He went up on the mountain by Himself to pray. Now when evening came, He was alone there"** (Matthew 14:23).

My personal experience would lead me to believe that if we do not desire to be alone with the Lord it could be an indication that something is indeed lacking in our relationship with Him. There might be a fear or reluctance to spend such time with the Lord because we know there are issues we have not wanted to face or think about. I believe another indication of this reluctance to get alone with the Lord may be seen when professed Christians always want to surround themselves with distractions—such as having the TV on in the background even if it is not being watched.

In addition, there is the pull of the internet which is not only a time stealer, but is also extremely dangerous without strict self-discipline to control its use—we need the fruit of the Holy Spirit which is self-control (Galatians 5:23). Even listening to something considered helpful and good such as Christian worship music can keep us from the quiet time of prayer and meditation alone with our Lord. The Psalmist prays, **"Remember how short my time is"** (Psalm 89:47). If we are not seeking the Lord now, when will we? Since Jesus practiced and obviously valued the importance of spending time alone with the Father to maintain and keep fresh His relationship with Him, how much more should we be willing to follow His example.

It all has to do with the state of our relationship with the Lord. In the scripture above from Second Corinthians Paul reminds his Christian readers that, **"Jesus Christ is in you?—unless indeed you are disqualified"** Accepting the last clause of this scripture at face value will be a challenge for some with certain theological backgrounds. But clearly unbelievers cannot go through a process of being disqualified or rejected because as persons unsaved they would *already* be positioned as disqualified and rejected. Jesus said, **"He who does not believe is condemned already, because he has not believed in the name of the only begotten Son of God"** (John 3:18). This is why it is so important we learn to be transparent and honest with Scripture. The adjective **"disqualified"** [KJV **"reprobate"**] (Greek, *adokimos*—rejected, worthless, castaway) in this context indicates someone who has lost their previous relationship with the Lord—even if an insincere one like that of Judas (See Acts 1:25). How could it mean anything else? One would have to impose some devious round-about semantics to try to make the words mean something different.

Salvation is a *relationship* that needs to be current with active, living, continuing faith. Let me reinforce this biblical truth once again: Salvation is a *relationship!* It is a relationship with the Lord that should be vibrant, alive, and continuous on a moment-by-moment basis. It begins when a person truly repents and believes in Jesus Christ and His atoning substitutionary sacrifice on the cross for his or her sins. This is generally known as being born again or being born from above as Jesus referred to it. In John 3:7 Jesus said, **"You must be born again"** (Greek: *anothen*—from above*).* This is where the journey of salvation begins, and it is when we experience for the first time a real spiritual connection with our wonderful Creator. It begins, continues, and ends with *believing.* Remember that Paul is writing to professed Christians who were members of the Church at Corinth. He called them **"saints"** (1 Corinthians 1:2). To be *rejected* would plainly mean that a spiritual connection had been broken. This is surely a solemn warning worthy of serious consideration—hence the need to *examine ourselves*. The truth is that a Christian's life should show some evidence of belief in the spiritual reality of the words, **"Jesus Christ is in you."** Also in Ephesians 3:17 Paul is likewise concerned, **"that Christ may dwell in your hearts through faith."** Jesus said, **"whoever believes"** (Greek is in the present continuous sense) will have **"everlasting life"** (John 3:16).

Many years ago I came to a realization through prayer and meditation in the Word that my faith in Christ's presence within me was at a superficial level. Over time I asked the Lord to help me by His Spirit to be more conscious of His presence within me as I lived through each day. Notice in the scripture above Paul writes that Christ should dwell or remain on a continual basis in our hearts **"through faith."** I learned the truth that I needed to exercise faith to experience daily the reality of Jesus' presence within me. How does faith come to us in order for us to experience this reality? Faith comes to us as a gift from God by the Spirit's implanting of it through the living Word of God which itself says, **"So then faith *comes* by hearing, and hearing by the word of God"** (Romans 10:17).

As I began to consciously put this into practice more regularly I found increased strength within me to live out my Christian testimony with more boldness. When we realize the awesome truth of His continuing presence dwelling within us in actual real time, we will begin to understand the incredible blessing of all the unlimited resources of God's love, peace and joy, which are available to us because of His real presence within us. This life-changing realization came to me in another way one day when meditating on Psalm 23:1 which says, **"The Lord is my Shepherd; I shall not want."** I suddenly understood that if the Lord is my shepherd and dwells within me with all His promises available to me through prayer and faith, what does **"I shall not want"** not cover? What it does cover is everything that is within the boundary of His will for us. This includes the truth that He has,

"Given to us exceedingly great and precious promises, that through these you may be partakers of the divine nature, having escaped the corruption *that is* **in the world though lust"** (2 Peter 1:4).

How many of us could say we have escaped the corruption of the world? The question we should ask ourselves is: Are we taking advantage of these great promises freely given to us through Christ so that we are entering into all that God has for us—including victory over the world, the flesh, and the devil? This would be a revived life would it not?

We remind visitors to our creation museum that the reason God created us was to enjoy a continual intimate relationship with Him. If we have not discovered this for ourselves, it must mean we have not yet entered by experience into the real purpose of our salvation. There should be a steady increase in the depth of our relationship with the Lord as we continue on in our salvation experience. There can be new levels of intimacy revealed to us as we continue in faith.

Our daily Christian walk should be far more than just attending church regularly, paying our tithes, and appearing to those in the world around us as *good people.* Jesus actually said, **"Woe to you when all men speak well of you"** (Luke 6:26). Our lives in Christ should spiritually affect those we rub shoulders with every day so they will either enjoy our presence or prefer to avoid our company. Not everyone is going to like us, and we should be prepared for this attitude from others. Not everyone liked Jesus! Paul uses the perfume that people put on their bodies or clothing as an illustration of our acceptance or rejection from others. He writes,

"Now thanks *be* to God who always leads us in triumph in Christ, and through us diffuses [or, manifests] **the fragrance of His knowledge in every place. For we are to God the fragrance of Christ among those who are being saved and among those who are perishing. To the one *we are* the aroma of death *leading* to death, and to the other the aroma of life *leading* to life"** (2 Corinthians 2:14-16).

Just as natural perfume can either attract or repel, so the presence of Christ through the indwelling of the Holy Spirit within us will cause people to either want to be around us, or prefer to avoid us. We should remember how people reacted to Jesus as recorded in the gospels. They either wanted to be with Him and listen to His teaching, or they wanted to attack Him and His message. Mark recorded, **"And the common people heard Him gladly"** (Mark 12:37). But we also read, **"And the scribes and chief priests heard it and sought how they might destroy Him; for they feared Him, because all the people were astonished at His teaching"** (Mark 11:18).

If we want our lives to count for God and be an influence for revival we can expect these types of responses. There are those who would like to destroy our creation museum ministry because we teach and support the truth of the Gospel. I know of a biblical creationist who has received death threats! Are we willing to suffer rejection from those who do not want to hear anything about God or the Gospel? As we seek to walk in close intimate fellowship with our Lord, are we willing to be rejected even by those we think of as our brothers and sisters in Christ? Yes, because this is most likely where much of the opposition to becoming revived and seeking God for revival will come from. The closer you draw nearer to God in intimate relationship, the lonelier and more isolated from those you thought of as friends you may find yourself becoming. However, the Lord will usually provide those who truly want God's best and will be true friends in fellowship with you as you seek God with all your heart. Would we really want any other kind of friends?

This close intimate relationship with God I am writing about will come at a cost. Christians who follow God wholeheartedly may be looked upon as out of step with the ordinary accepted way of living and doing things. As some would put it, such a dedicated follower of Christ is *marching to the beat of a different drum!* It calls for radically living out the challenging teachings of Jesus without reserve. Consider these words of our Lord:

Then Jesus said to His disciples, "If anyone desires to come after Me, let him deny himself, and take up his cross, and follow Me. For whoever desires to save his life will lose it, but whoever loses his life for My sake will find it. For what profit is it to a man if he gains the whole world, and loses his own soul? Or what will a man give in exchange for his soul?" (Matthew 16:24-26).

In order to become personally revived and have our lives affect those around us for revival, we can expect the Holy Spirit to lead us to spend hours in earnest prayer. This would be like the woman and the unjust judge mentioned earlier, when the women was building up her case by her continual persistent demand. God is looking for *real* faith, and we must remember that His timing and answers to our requests are always under His control. We have to confront ourselves with the decision as to whether we are willing to undergo personal sacrifice of time and energy to seek the Lord. We may find the Lord impressing us with the desire to forego pleasant legitimate activities with which we could have spent our time. Remember that Jesus purposefully left the enjoyment of fellowship with His disciples on many occasions for the more needful time spent in communion with His Father. The truth is, as many dedicated followers of our Lord have discovered, the more we engage in the work of ministry the more we will desire to do so.

As we grow closer to the Lord in our personal relationship we should expect to see the presence of the Lord within us impacting those around us. Evangelist Smith Wigglesworth, whom we mentioned in chapter 13 shared one of his experiences as follows:

> On another occasion Wigglesworth boarded a train at Bradford to travel to London. He selected a corner seat. Eventually, five more people joined him in the compartment. As was his custom, he took out his Testament and began to read and pray silently. He never spoke a word to his fellow travelers.
>
> About thirty miles away from London he went to the rest room. As he was making his way back to the compartment, the man who had been sitting next to him said, "I don't know what it was, but when I sat next to you, a terrible fear gripped me. I was afraid I was going to die. What was it?" . . . All the others there said they had experienced the same feeling. Wigglesworth explained to them about conviction and the way of salvation. They all knelt on the floor of the compartment and accepted the Lord (Smith Wigglesworth, *The Secret of His Power,* Harrison House, Tulsa, Oklahoma, 1982 37).

Wigglesworth lived with a close moment-by-moment relationship with the Lord which others, even unbelievers, were often able to sense. This is surely a challenge to all of us today if we realize that our daily living and testimony for Jesus apparently leaves people unaffected. One thing we can know for sure, if we do not seek the Lord until we are having a continual intimate personal relationship with Him, we should not expect to have experiences anything like those of Wigglesworth. It was because of his close relationship with the Lord that the power of the Holy Spirit was able to minister through him to others. God is not a respecter of persons, and has provided wonderful gifts for ministry which the Holy Spirit will minister through us if we will seek the Lord diligently (See 1 Corinthians 12 for a partial list of spiritual gifts).

It is hard for me to imagine anything more awesome than having the presence of almighty God residing within me by the Holy Spirit. Jesus told His disciples at one point that this special relationship would be theirs in the future. He said,

"He who believes in Me, as the Scripture has said, out of his heart [belly, KJV] will flow rivers of living water." But this He spoke concerning the Spirit, whom those believing in Him would receive; for the Holy Spirit was not yet given, because Jesus was not yet glorified (John 7:38,39).

This is what personal revival is, and this is exactly how it can spread to others as a flowing river from one person to another. But notice the condition required before the fulfillment of the promise, **"he who believes in Me."** The emphasis is always on present-active faith. In Hebrews 11:6 it says, **"But without faith *it is* impossible to please *Him*, for he who comes to God must believe that He is, and *that* He is a rewarder**

of those who diligently seek Him." Believe, believe, and believe— this is what God is looking for. Pursue the right relationship with the Lord, and your relationship and witness to others will be powerful.

CHAPTER 17
EXTREME SACRIFICE?

Will the blessing of revival coming to communities across America require extreme sacrifice on the part of believers? For some I believe so, because it will likely come with severe persecution. Are you willing to die for your Lord? Can you honestly say you would gladly lay down your life for the cause of the Gospel? Would you also be willing to sacrifice your life for another (whether a Christian or an unbeliever) when under a situation of persecution? Do we value our lives as Christians in the here and now more than the future reality of being in the presence of the Lord?

Heavy questions? Yes. Preservation of our physical lives on this earth for as long as possible is naturally something dear to us. However, I don't think these are things the average Christian wants to think about too often—the inexorable certainty and end of our physical lives. Yet, millions of believers around the world have had to face such real-life challenging trials, and many are in situations of severe persecution at this very hour.

For all of us, death is a certainty whether it comes to us earlier or later. How we think about it will mirror the condition of our relationship with the Lord. Can we consider it with a sense of peace in our hearts knowing we are secure in our relationship with Him? Or, do we tend to avoid thinking about it because it makes us feel uncomfortable. These reactions would be an indication of the level of intimate fellowship and closeness (or not) we have with God in our daily lives. To begin with, I believe it will help if we can get an understanding of where we stand in our relationship with the Lord by dwelling on the meaning of the word *love* from a spiritual perspective. Here is a true statement: *Where my love is, is where my heart is.* Do we genuinely love our times of fellowship with the Lord in prayer and meditation of the Word without reservation? Do we love and value Christian friendship and fellowship? Do we love to give generously of our finances and resources for the Lord's work? Are we willing to give of our time and show love to those who desire our attention, even though such persons may not appeal to us naturally as those we would like to associate with too closely? Here's a test Jesus gives us to help us evaluate ourselves,

"If anyone comes to Me and does not hate his father and mother, wife and children, brothers and sisters, yes, and his own life also, he cannot be My disciple" (Luke 14:26).

At first this seems too hard and even unreasonable a saying for people to live up to in reality. It appears natural to us, and rightly so, that our earthly relationships of family and friends should have our unconditional love and care above all others. Yes, but above the Lord? No! If we give our earthly relationships priority over our relationship with the Lord we have got it wrong!

The truth about this may be a surprising revelation to many of us in spite of what we think. Because if we love our family more than God we will not be loving them with the God-like purity of love we could and should! It will likely be a selfish, narcissistic relationship for the purpose of the enjoyment we get out of it for ourselves. But if we love God first and foremost, as the scripture says, **"You shall love the LORD your God with all your heart, with all your soul, and with all your mind"** (Matthew 22:37), then it follows that the pure and genuine love of God should naturally be the overflow from our lives first to our family, and then to those we interact with on a daily basis. The Ten Commandments begin with, **"You shall have no other gods before Me"** (Exodus 20:3). The obvious reason for this commandment is because if we have another god it would be a false one, and would put us in dangerous territory spiritually. The danger of having false gods is the conflict they would cause with our relationship to the true God.

Jesus uses the word *hate* in the scripture above in the sense of *loving less*. Of course we are to love our family and friends. But our family, especially those precious grandchildren, can be as gods to us if we are not careful. I believe the general order of the expression of love flowing from or lives should be God first, family second—along with special love for the family of God, and then love for all others. Will this involve sacrifice of our personal time, physical energy, financial resources, and personal preferences? You can be sure it will.

But is it really a sacrifice to love God first and foremost above all others? How can we intelligently think such a thing when we consider what the Lord has done for us? How could we even begin to compare any sacrifice or inconvenience we experience during our lives with how Jesus suffered and bled on the cross to obtain eternal salvation and future blessings beyond compare? No, we should be only too willing to give our all for Him after all He has done in the past and continues to do for us.

Every morning we should say to ourselves, **"This is the day the Lord has made; we will rejoice and be glad in it"** (Psalm 118:23). We should remember again that we can pray, **"Give us this day our daily bread"** (Matthew 6:11), and offer thanksgiving with grateful hearts for all His wonderful provision for our lives. Yes, if we truly love God as we should it will change our perception of life and how we can be led of God to help others find Him and live with a spirit of revival.

We can even love our enemies! Jesus said it, so it must be possible. However, we are certainly not required to love our enemy Satan, for he is working to deceive as many as possible and lead them away from a relationship with God to eternal destruction. Satan's influence has produced some extremely evil people in this world, but we are told to pray for such since there is always the possibility of change and salvation if they repent and believe. Since the new American administration began under president Trump in 2017, we are seeing the exposure of blatant hypocrisy, hatred, immorality, and lack of unity for the good of the country among many of our elected leaders as well as the media. We should be praying for the exposure of such things. This could certainly be an unexpected answer to prayer by laying a foundation of spiritual hunger and discontent in preparation for a revival move of God to spread across communities of our country. Here are the amazing words of Jesus giving us our *modus operandi* which is contrary to the normal instincts of human nature:

"You have heard that it was said, '*You shall love your neighbor* and hate your enemy.' But I say to you, love your enemies, bless those who curse you, do good to those who hate you, and pray for those who spitefully use you and persecute you, that you may be sons of your Father in heaven" (Matthew 5:43-45).

It is just not a natural expression of humanity to love those who hate us. I learned the principle many years ago that two opposing negatives do not produce a positive! However, if there is a humble conciliatory attitude with God's supernatural love and wisdom emanating from one side of a conflict, there surely must be the possibility of a harmonious solution. It is not a sign of weakness to love those who hate us, but of strength. Such strength can only come from within a person by the presence of the Holy Spirit. The first fruit of the Holy Spirit mentioned is *love* (Galatians 5:22). The question we need to face is: Are we willing to be that person who responds to those who hate us, not with like-minded antagonism, but with the love and wisdom of God? Are we willing to sacrifice our own comfort level in order to see the Spirit of God work in the lives of others—even those who love to hate us?

It may seem like an extreme sacrifice asked of us, but this is our calling as disciples of Christ. We need to remember that the foundational reason why we as Christians are hated is because those who hate us are being deceived by the great deceiver, Satan. Therefore, the complete misunderstanding of Christians by unbelievers is because of a spiritual disconnect. The unsaved in the media and those among the intellectual elite are perfect examples of this. The Bible says, **"But the natural man does not receive the things of the Spirit of God, for they are foolishness to him; nor can he know *them*, because they are spiritually discerned"** (1 Corinthians 2:14).

There is an old expression, sometimes mockingly spoken of those who have become new believers which says: He (or she) has seen the light. It's a good description because it fits what happens to people when they experience the reality of what it means to be saved and forgiven. They have seen, spiritually, the light of God who is light. No longer are they stumbling around in meaningless darkness not knowing where they are going. Jesus spoke of the contrast between light and darkness when He said, **"Walk while you have the light, lest darkness overtake you; he who walks in darkness does not know where he is going"** (John 12:35). He also said, **"I am the light of the world. He who follows Me shall not walk in darkness, but have the light of life"** (John 8:12).

Yet, so many are walking through life with no hope or plan for the ultimate future. God does have a plan for His people—every one of us. The question is, are we finding that God-ordained individual purpose for our existence as believers? Of course, if we are not keeping up our relationship with God through prayer and feeding on the Word, then we will be in a state of limbo, and our daily experience will be that of just going through the motions of whatever we do. Yes, we can be professed Christians and at the same time be bored and unfulfilled in life. How tragic, when fullness of purpose and joy is meant to be providing excitement and fulfillment as we go through each day. But instead, life may not seem too different from that which we experienced before becoming a believer.

It may be difficult for many of us to remember our self-conscious condition before we first came into relationship with the Lord. Looking back to that time for myself it seems to have been similar to living life as in a dream. Each day would come and go with its activities and demands that I understood were expected of me. My father was quite strict and made it clear what my behavioral boundaries were. Regarding spiritual awareness, I knew I believed in God in a foggy sort of way, but I was basically just a typical young person shaped by the particular culture in which I was being raised. It was not until I believed the Gospel, repented of my sins, asked God to forgive me and be the guiding light of my life, that I began to discern a sense of focus, direction, and purpose for my existence.

Many of you reading this will probably identify with similar experiences in your own journey to becoming a child of God. Remembering our own journey could help us to identify with the spiritually unsaved. It should give us understanding on ways to approach the unbeliever with the love of God through our thoughts, words, and actions as we share the truth with them. We are expected to witness the truth of the Gospel by, **"speaking the truth in love"** (Ephesians 4:15). This, of course, is often not easy. In my book *Can I Be Pure?: Holy Living in a Corrupt World,* I gave a short vignette of a situation I had seen in my own experience as follows:

> Pete walked over to the break table in the pressroom at the print shop where he worked. Almost immediately the off-color stories and jokes began to flow. It was hard not to laugh when everyone else was laughing. Pete wished he had the courage to say something that would turn the conversation to better things. He was a Christian, but had never mentioned it to his coworkers, and always tried to avoid the subject of religion (Rod Butterworth, *Can I Be Pure?: Holy Living in a Corrupt World,* Createspace, Amazon Books, 2017 12).

Yes, the pressures we experience in the secular world can intimidate us into silence when we should be speaking. I gave the title *Extreme Sacrifice?* to this chapter because I believe as Christians we should be willing to undergo extreme sacrifice if we are called to do so. We can think of many saints from the Scriptures who underwent extreme sacrifice for their faithful service of the Lord. For example, Noah, Moses, Joseph, Isaiah, Jeremiah, John the Baptist, Stephen, Paul, and the Apostle John. In the history of America we Christians have not suffered such sacrifices by comparison so far, but we would be on shaky ground if we think we are immune to such a scenario. We have had a pretty easy road to travel with the freedom to express our Christian beliefs and practices, but while we were enjoying this freedom the enemy has been coming in with increasingly more bold attacks against our Judeo-Christian foundation. We are, in fact, in a battle for the very existence of biblical Christianity in these teen years of the twenty-first century. It reminds me of the situation in the prophet Jeremiah's day when the people were moving away from serving God and being obedient to His Word. Jeremiah was called as a prophet of God to deliver a very difficult message to the people of Israel, and it got him into trouble with ungodly men. We read,

"Therefore thus says the Lord concerning the men of Anathoth who seek your life, saying 'Do not prophesy in the name of the Lord, lest you die by our hand'" (Jeremiah 11:21).

Death threats? Yes. For example, biblical creationist Ken Ham has received death threats because he teaches God is real, the Bible is the Word of God, and evolution is not supported by real science. Because of the craziness of political correctness Christians are being told they cannot mention words like God, Jesus, Bible, and witness the truth of the Gospel in the marketplace. However, as a nation we still exist under the guidelines of the American Constitution which legally guarantees freedom of speech, and regardless of attempts to impose limits on Christians, we have the legal right to speak our faith. This is when extreme personal sacrifice may be a factor for Christians today, as it was in the lives of the early disciples when they were commanded by ungodly religious leaders to cease preaching Jesus as savior and healer. Peter and John gave their answer which is an example for us to follow today. We read,

"But Peter and John answered and said to them, 'Whether it is right in the sight of God to listen to you more than to God, you judge. For we cannot but speak the things which we have seen and heard'" (Acts 4:19,20).

I wonder how many of us would have the boldness of Peter if our Constitutional protections were legally abrogated. It wasn't long before Peter found himself in prison, and King Herod was demonically influenced to attack the Church by having him put to death. Peter was willing to suffer extreme sacrifice as a faithful disciple of Jesus, and if we are serious about doing something positive for revival in America we should have a similar mindset. Are you ready for the possibility of extreme sacrifice?

CHAPTER 18

WHAT WILL WE CHOOSE?

Surely the most terrifying words anyone could hear from God on the Day of Judgment would be, **"I never knew you; depart from Me, you who practice lawlessness!"** (Matthew 7:23). These words were pronounced by Jesus when He was teaching on the importance of knowing people for who they really are.

The Apostle John wrote of, **"many deceivers have gone out into the world who do not confess Jesus Christ *as* coming in the flesh. This is the deceiver and an antichrist. Look to yourselves, that we do not lose those things we worked for, but *that* we may receive a full reward"** (2 John 7,8). So with these warnings in mind we must be careful how we are influenced, and we must seek God's help to discern the real motives and *fruits* evident in the lives of those who profess to be ministering for God. Under the wrong influence there is the possibility for any of us to be led astray and, **"lose those things we worked for."** Visible ministry through meetings, missions, books, evangelism, and media exposure, may look good on the surface. But what is God really looking for? Giving us a fuller picture Jesus said,

"Therefore by their fruits you will know them. Not everyone who says to Me, 'Lord, Lord,' shall enter the kingdom of heaven, but he who does the will of My Father in heaven.

Many will say to Me in that day, 'Lord, Lord, have we not prophesied in Your name, cast out demons in Your name, and done many wonders in Your name?' And then I will declare to them, 'I

never knew you; depart from Me, you who practice lawlessness!"

These solemn words from Jesus would make me want to examine my spiritual state carefully and evaluate how God sees me from His perspective. I believe the answer to the question of what God is looking for is found in these words, **"I never knew you."** From the Garden of Eden on we see that God wanted to spend time with His creation—not animal life, but human life, Adam and Eve. This is because humans are created in the image of God. **"Then God said, 'Let Us make man in Our image, according to Our likeness"** (Genesis 1:26). God had a personal intimate relationship with Adam and Eve and spoke to them as recorded, **"Then God blessed them, and God said to them, 'Be fruitful and multiply; fill the earth and subdue it"** (Genesis 1:28). That God spent time with Adam and Eve every day is implied by the words, **"And they heard the sound of the Lord God walking in the garden in the cool of the day"** (Genesis 3:8).

Initially, Adam and Eve knew God personally in a similar way (but more spiritually pure) to the people we know in our families and circle of acquaintances today. We speak to people, we share thoughts with them, we share time with them and go places with them, and we interact with them in a variety of ways. In a spiritual sense, this is exactly what God wants today. Above all other things, He wants that personal intimate relationship of *knowing Him* and walking in fellowship with Him. He wants to teach us more about Himself, but we must choose whether this is what we want or not. This is how the Apostle Paul expressed the desire of his heart with these words,

"That I may gain Christ and be found in Him, not having my own righteousness, which *is* from

the law, but that which *is* through faith in Christ, the righteousness which is from God by faith; that I may know Him and the power of His resurrection, and the fellowship of His sufferings, being conformed to His death" (Philippians 3:8-10).

Did the Apostle Paul **"know Him"**? As Christians we would surely think Paul knew Christ in a personal relationship far deeper than most of us experience today. Yet, he had a continual desire to know Him more. Do we have the same desire today? It is a choice we are free to make or not to make. Right after Jesus said, **"I never knew you; depart from Me"** He said,

"Therefore whoever hears these saying of Mine, and does them, I will liken him to a wise man who built his house on the rock: and the rain descended, the floods came, and the winds blew and beat on that house; and it did not fall, for it was founded on the rock. But everyone who hears these sayings of Mine, and does not do them, will be like a foolish man who built his house on the sand: and the rain descended, the floods came, and the winds blew and beat on that house; and it fell. And great was its fall." (Matthew 7:24-27).

We are blest to *hear* so much of the Word of God in America. Jesus said that *hearing* is only the first part, but it is the *doing* that is absolutely vital to the success of our lives as believers desiring to be His obedient servants. What should we do? We should be *doing* the sayings of Jesus. If we fail to put into practice the sayings of Jesus we may be trying to build the house of our Christianity on sinking sand! What are the sayings of Jesus? Here are some of them from the pen of Matthew:

"Repent, for the kingdom of heaven is at hand" (Matthew 4:17).

"Follow Me, and I will make you fishers of men" (Matthew 4:19).

"Rejoice [when persecuted] and be exceedingly glad, for great *is* your reward in heaven, for so they persecuted the prophets who were before you" (Matthew 5:12).

"Let you light so shine before men, that they may see your good works and glorify your Father in heaven" (Matthew 5:16).

"I say to you, love your enemies, bless those who curse you, do good to those who hate you, and pray for those who spitefully use you and persecute you" (Matthew 5:44).

"Take heed that you do not do your charitable deeds before men, to be seen of them" (Matthew 6:1).

"When you pray, go into your room, and when you have shut your door, pray to your Father who *is* in the secret *place*; and your Father who sees in secret will reward you openly" (Matthew 6:6).

"When you fast, anoint your head and wash your face, so that you do not appear to men to be fasting" (Matthew 6:17,18).

"Lay up for yourselves treasures in heaven, where neither moth nor rust destroy and where thieves do not break in and steal" (Matthew 6:20).

"Do not worry about your life, what you will eat or what you will drink; nor about your body, what you will put on" (Matthew 6:25).

"But seek first the kingdom of God and His

righteousness, and all these things will be added to you" (Matthew 6:33).

"**Judge** [or condemn] **not, that you be not judged**" (Matthew 7:1).

"Ask, and it will be given to you; seek, and you will find; knock, and it will be opened to you" Matthew 7:7).

"Pray the Lord of the harvest to send out laborers into His harvest" (Matthew 9:38).

"Whatever I tell you in the dark, speak in the light; and what you hear in the ear, preach on the housetops" (Matthew 10:27).

"And he who does not take his cross and follow after Me is not worthy of Me" (Matthew 10:38).

"Come to Me, all *you* who labor and are heavy laden, and I will give you rest" (Matthew 11:28).

"Take heed that you do not despise one of these little ones, for I say to you that in heaven their angels see the face of My Father who is in heaven" (Matthew 18:10).

"Let the little children come to Me, and do not forbid them; for of such is the kingdom of heaven" (Matthew 19:14).

"Whoever desires to become great among you, let him be your servant" (Matthew 20:27).

"And whatever things you ask in prayer, believing, you will receive" (Matthew 21:22).

"You shall love the Lord your God with all your heart, with all your soul, and with all your mind. This is the first and great commandment, and *the* second is like it: You shall love your neighbor as yourself" (Matthew 22:37-39).

"Watch therefore, for you know neither the day nor the hour in which the Son of Man is coming" (Matthew 25:13).

"Watch and pray, lest you enter into temptation" (Matthew 26:41).

"Go therefore and make disciples of all nations, baptizing them in the name of the Father and of the Son and of the Holy Spirit, teaching them to observe all things that I have commanded you; and lo, I am with you always, *even* to the end of the age" (Matthew 28:19,20).

Lest some think we are in danger of elevating outward works in order to keep our relationship with God, let us be reminded that obeying God in these things is part of our responsibility as disciples of Christ. Jesus said, **"This is the work of God, that you believe in Him whom He sent"** (John 6:29). And if we truly *believe* in Him and His sayings we will want to please Him by willing obedience. If we continue in a living vital moment-by-moment relationship with the Lord our salvation is assured.

So the Lord gives us the choice: Revival or Rejection! Each of us has a part to play in the future of America. Again, what is one of the most important things we should be doing to bring revival among God's people and effective witness to unbelievers who are around us? It is to pray, and pray, and pray, with the earnestness and compassion of Jesus for those wandering in spiritual darkness. During an interview with Pastor Robert Jeffries of Dallas, Texas, he said the following and included a quote from W. A. Criswell:

"The only way to change the direction of America is by changing the hearts of Americans," Jeffries observed. Calling Christians to a renewed emphasis on personal evangelism, Jeffries quoted the words of his predecessor, Dr. W. A. Criswell, who 35 years ago observed what was and is needed in America, "The nation cannot turn to God if *I* do not turn to God. The nation cannot repent if *I* do not repent. God doesn't win nations or companies or crowds or throngs; He wins *souls*—one by one. And the only way we can lift our nation Godward is if *I* am moved Godward."

(Robert Jeffries, www.charismanews.com/politics/opinion/ accessed 10-27-17).

Notice the italicized "*I*" which Dr. Criswell wanted to emphasize in his quote. He puts the course of action squarely upon us—each of us individually. Again, God's Word says, **"Draw near to God and He will draw near to you"** (James 4:8). We are losing the battle if we think we can be spectators only in this spiritual warfare. Our enemy, Satan, is not alarmed by professed Christians who stand on the sidelines hoping other Christians will fight the good fight of faith for them. May we be willing to accept and to choose the privilege of being His servants as we enter into His service with joy and faith.

"If you can believe, all things *are* possible to him who believes" (Mark 9:23).

You can find more of Rod Butterworth's books at:

www.butterworthpublications.com

Also at Amazon Books.

Proof

Made in the USA
Columbia, SC
10 January 2018